MAGIC'S
MOST AMAZING
STORIES

A COLLECTION of INCREDIBLE STORIES

FROM WORLD FAMOUS MAGICIANS

compiled by Award-Winning Magician Ivan Amodei

Published by Eclipse P&D, Inc.

Magic's Most Amazing Stories
A Collection of Incredible Stories from World Famous Magicians
Copyright © 2009 Eclipse P&D, Inc. & Ivan Amodei.

First soft cover edition printed 2009, volume 1

ISBN 10: 0-615-31250-7
ISBN 13: 978-0-615-31250-7

First published and printed in the United States of America by:
Eclipse P&D, Inc.
5220 Gabbert Road
Moorpark, California 93021 USA

Book Design: Ivan Amodei (www.ivanamodei.com)
Layout & Production: Ivan Amodei
Cover & Back Cover Design: Ivan Amodei
Illustrations: Karen Boyle (www.karendoylesart.com)
About the Author: Jonathan Levit (www.jonathanlevit.com)
Proofreading/Editing: Shawn McMaster (www.conjuredupcreations.com),
Ivan Amodei & Jennifer Amodei (www.amodeidesigns.com)

Acknowledgments

I want to *Thank* everyone that gave me permission and/or contributed a story for my book. In alphabetical order: *Aldo Colombini, Alfonso, Anders Moden, Asi Wind, Avani Mehta, Ben Jackson, Bill Wisch, Bruce Gold, Carl Andrews, Christopher Hart, Chris Randall, Dan McKinnon, Dana Daniels, Daniel Sylvester, Danny Cole, Dave Cox, David Minkin, Dennis Loomis, Dick Barry, Doc Eason, Doug Gorman, Ed Alonzo, Eric Decamps, Gay Blackstone, Gazzo, Gene Anderson, George Saterial, George Schindler, Gerry Katzman, Goldfinger & Dove, Howard Hamburg, Jason Latimer, Jeff Hobson, Jennifer Amodei, Jim Bentley, John George, Kostya Kimlat, Curtis Kam, Mac King, Marc Bachrach, Matt Marcy, Max Maven, Michael Close, Michael Finney, Milt Larsen, Murray Sawchuck, Nick Lewin, Peter Samelson, R. Paul Wilson, Rachel Colombini, Rich Marotta, Richard Turner, Rick Merrill, Rob Rasner, Rob Zabrecky, Rocco Silano, Ron Wilson, Shawn Farquhar, Shawn McMaster, Simon Lovell, Stephen Bargatze, Steve Cohen, Steve Dacri, TC Tahoe, Tim Ellis, Tom Burgoon, Tom Ogden, Tony Binarelli and Woody Pittman.*

I would also like to *Thank* Karen Boyle for the fantastic illustrations. *Thank you* to my good friend Shawn McMaster for all the great edits, glitch-catching, grammatical tips and advice. Another *Thank you* to my good friend Jonathan Levit for the fantastic design tips & tricks, as well as, writing the "*About the Author*" piece on *page 251*. Finally, huge *Thank You* to my wife Jennifer for her help with story writing, research, editing and phone calls. There would not be a book today without everyone's contribution listed here.

Thank you all so very much.
Ivan Amodei
December 2009

INTRODUCTION

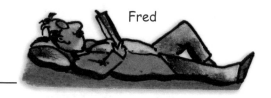

Fred

It was around 1:00am. The hustle of the nights activity at the World Famous Magic Castle in Hollywood, CA was coming to a close. I had just finished doing my sets, and I met up with some fellow magician friends at the bar.

Like a scene out of the glory days of the rat pack, sharing *story* after *story* of the crazy, funny moments that come with the art of performing as a professional magician. That night on my way home, I thought, *"I have to document these stories."*

However, it is *not* my intention to reveal trade secrets here. I do hope though, to make known, the passion and dedication we all share as artists for our craft. This book will give you an inside look into the *crazy* things that happen to us while we work. You'll instantly feel a part of this underground world.

It is also much more than just leafing through incredible tales. There are life lessons inside. I hope that all my peers and the legends in this book know how grateful I am for their stories. I also hope that this is a proper tribute to their work and dedication to an art we all respect and love so much.

I have an enormous amount of reverence for this art and its members. It continues to motivate me to reach for the stars, try *even* harder, and *always* keep dreaming.♦

So how do you read this book? You'll most likely jump around quite a bit and not read this *cover-to-cover* like other books. I placed *random* story snippets all throughout it. Some excerpts might immediately catch your interest, and you'll find yourself jumping over read that full story right away.

The *Contents* in the front allow you to find which **Magician** to read about. Here you'll also find the *"story title"* and page number. Some magicians also have more than one story.

The *Credits & Acknowledgements* start *on page 252* and act like an **Index**. It is sorted alphabetically by the contributor's first name — and in (**red**). You'll quickly find the person who **contributed the story**, for example, (*as told by Ivan Amodei*) and which story(s) they provided.

Let our clumsy magician *"Fred"* take you on a fun ride through the book. Get your family and friends together and have everyone take turns reading their favorite tale(s). Just sit back and listen — it's a fantastic way to absorb this book.

To sum up, the stories inside are **amazing** — hence the title. I hope you enjoy this anthology, as much as, I loved putting it together. The next few hours are going to be a blast. Enjoy!

Ivan Amodei

CONTENTS

CONTENTS

Contents

CONTENTS

Dedicated to my children Julia & Christiano,
who are proof that miracles do happen.

chapter
one

WHAT PARROT?

DANA DANIELS

AS TOLD BY DANA DANIELS

I developed a plan when traveling with my Parrot Luigi, at least when I traveled by air. I would untuck my shirt and place Luigi on my rear end, letting the back of my shirt conceal him.

I'd walk through the airport with the Parrot hanging behind me. He wouldn't set off any alarms, he's a bird. Afterwards, I'd go into a bathroom and put him back into his cage, which looked like a *carry-on* bag. Very sneaky. No one was any the wiser.

Once after a show in a freezing cold Columbus, Ohio, I arrived at the airport wearing a trench coat. Rather than employing my regular *hang-loose* method of sneaking Luigi onto the plane, I decided to put him into a huge trench coat pocket. I proceed through the entire ticket line with lots of people all around me. When I arrived up front, the ticket agent was clicking away on his computer. He looked up at me and said, *"One bag to check in?"* I replied, *"Yes sir."* Then he said, *"You want to check in the Parrot?"*

Now, I'm looking directly at this guy and I thought, *"How does he know I have a Parrot?"* Did he see my show last night? Does he recognize me? I was totally confused. So I blew it off and said, *"What Parrot?"* He stopped typing, looked up at me again and replied, *"The one on your shoulder!"* Stunned, I thought, *"Oh my God …No!"*

Slowly, I looked over to my left shoulder and, YES, Luigi was right there. Apparently, while I was waiting in line, he crawled out of my pocket, climbed up my back and arrived on my shoulder. I immediately thought, *"Now what am I going to do?"* There's no way he's going to let me on this plane. **Humor**, I thought, was my only way out of this mess, so I responded, with a straight face, *"Oh no, he's just here to see me off."* The guy totally lost it and burst out laughing. As he finished the paperwork, I thought, *"Man, I'm in big trouble!"* But he handed me my ticket and said, *"Here you go Mr. Daniels. Have a safe trip."* I walked off with the Luigi on my shoulder and my head in my chest — just mortified.

Before I went through security, I put Luigi back on my butt, crossed my fingers, held my breath and pretended like nothing ever happened. ♦

> GOD, NO!

FAREWELL

ROB ZABRECKY

AS TOLD BY ROB ZABRECKY

IT'S FOR AN EXTREMELY HIGH-PROFILE CLIENT

I am an entertainer with lots of obsessions: tap dancing, The Carpenters, avant-garde music, and pop singer Michael Jackson. It was in February, 2009 after performing magic in some nightclubs of Tokyo, I returned to Los Angeles and faced the sort of uncertain financial future common to most professional entertainers.

On the morning of February 21st my phone rang. It was a producer friend with a very interesting proposition. *"It's a gig performing for a major celebrity, and it's a birthday party. Today."*

I declined. I had a busy day ahead, with a couple of television commercial auditions followed by a night performing at The Magic Castle. *"You should consider it,"* he countered. *"It will be an interesting afternoon. It's for an extremely high-profile client."*

I took the bait and asked whom, and admit I was stunned when I was told the gig was for Michael Jackson. I couldn't get the word *"YES"* out fast enough. I was instructed to be at Jackson's Beverly Hills home in three hours. I would be performing at a birthday party for Jackson's 7 year-old son, *"Blanket,"* as part of a variety show.

It seemed unreal. I kissed my first girl inside Glendale's Moonlight Roller Rink back in the late 1970s while Jackson's *OFF THE WALL* played on the sound system. I've always been fascinated by him. Throughout the years I would periodically turn to my wife and ask, *"What do you think Michael Jackson is doing right now?"* Musically he lost me at *BAD*, but what became more important was the evolution of his character and the strangeness of him. I couldn't wait to see what he was going to do next. The whole idea of meeting him was just dreamlike. I had no idea what I was even going to see.

Jackson's house was off Sunset Boulevard in the affluent Holmby Hills neighborhood. I arrived and found people gathered outside the property. I thought they were performers, but it became apparent that they were actually fans waiting for a glimpse of their idol.

I approached the home and they accosted me, asking what was happening inside. I pushed past to a large metal gate. I could see several security guards in suits on the other side. I announced myself and the gates opened.

The thing that struck me as odd was that there were two big Christmas wreaths on the gate, and it was already late February. Someone should have tossed them in the trash. They were totally dead. I was ushered inside and the guards demanded my phone, which I reluctantly gave them. I glanced around and was surprised by what I saw. It was your typical Beverly Hills mansion, but the thing I noticed right away was that it didn't look cared for. The landscaping was neglected and having seen pictures of Neverland and his Encino house. I was a little surprised by this. The plants all looked like they could use a good watering. I, along with a few other performers were kept in a room to the side of the house. I could see a large backyard with a swimming pool. I turned to Matt Plendl, one of the world's finest Hula-Hoop men who was also performing, and asked if the whole thing seemed kind of strange. *"Honey, this is the weirdest,"* Matt replied.

I was informed I would go on second, after a juggler. We were told we would perform next to the pool, and the audience would be seated in four lounge chairs already setup. It was then that we realized there would be no guests — just Jackson and his three children. It felt kind of sad. No friends, no balloons or birthday cake. As walkie-talkies buzzed, the four of them suddenly appeared,

HONEY, THIS IS THE WEIRDEST!

heading toward the pool. They looked just like a family of ducks. Michael was leading with the kids following, from tallest to smallest. He was wearing black-satin pajamas and looked fragile. The kids looked surprisingly normal. They seemed like a happy little family, which I wasn't expecting. They were all smiling.

When the juggler finished, I headed down to take his place. I noticed another dying Christmas wreath, on a door of the pool house. I thought that was a little odd, but the whole place had a slight feel of neglect. I kept fixing things with my eyes. As I reached the pool, I saw this little broken-down pirate ship floating in the water, knocking against the tile. It really resonated with me.

The symbolism of the wrecked pirate ship and the Peter Pan/Neverland connection has left an indelible mark

in my mind ever since Jackson and the kids began to giggle as I approached in my black suit and off-kilter performing persona. Jackson was wearing his trademark fedora and sunglasses and only his jaw line was visible.

They seemed to enjoy the magic show, but after a few minutes, a paparazzi helicopter appeared overhead. The kids immediately recoiled, each of them pulling a cloth veil over his or her head. I stopped. The kids remained hidden for about 30 seconds until the helicopter left, and then everything returned to the way it had been.

They seemed to view the helicopter as some sort of pervasive and evil force. Blanket especially. It appeared to be like some sort of strange air raid. I resumed

> **MJ DEAD — TURN ON RADIO!**

my act and was pleased to see Jackson and the kids laughing at the right beats. But as I began a monologue about being different and an outsider, while cutting out paper dolls, one with two heads, I realized I'd lost them.

I thought they would love it and think I was hitting an empathetic chord for knowing how they felt, but they were just staring at me blankly. It was obvious that they didn't understand.

I think it was just totally outside their experience. I was talking about neighbors and being the weird boy next door, and they have probably never even had neighbors. They live totally insulated lives. I moved into

my shrinking-card finale and they were with me again, laughing and clapping. Even the security guards seemed to be enjoying the show. When I finished, Jackson and the kids applauded enthusiastically, thanked me and told me the show was great. As I walked away, I was elated. I had just performed for Michael Jackson, and at that moment I knew exactly what he was doing! Then, just four months later, while driving back from Las Vegas with two magician friends. We passed through Barstow and my wife suddenly text the shocking message: *"MJ dead — turn on radio — so SAD."* I immediately switched on the radio just as the announcers were confirming that Jackson was indeed dead. It didn't seem real, and it was very sad.

He seemed like someone who was probably at the end of his musical career, but the family life seemed surprisingly light, from what I saw.

He might not have been the King of Pop anymore, but the four of them seemed like peas in a pod — an army of four – and I wondered what would happen to them without him. ♦

Did You Know?

HOUDINI

Houdini's house in NYC is still standing, and still sports the custom inlaid floor tiles with Houdini's HH initials.

Reno 911!

Murray Sawchuck

As Told by Murray Sawchuck

I was booked on the Comedy Central show *Reno 911!*, as a guest star. I played a magician driving under the influence. Since it was the first show, and because it was never on TV before, no one knew the characters, the actors or even the story line.

I arrived on set, blue-suit in hand, magic props and all. As I walked down the sidewalk to my trailer, I passed an peculiar looking security guard. He seemed a bit out of place. Politely, he nodded to me, so I nodded to him.

I was in SHOCK! This security guard was wearing *SUPER, SUPER tight, shorty, shorts* with socks pulled up high above his knees. So tight, I could tell what religion he was. I thought to myself, *"This is a fashion Hindenburg!"* We were, however, shooting in Hollywood,

A SECURITY GUARD WEARING SUPER, SUPER TIGHT, SHORTY SHORTS!

CA, so anything goes I guess. I looked at my friend and with a snide wisecrack remarked, *"Wow!!! That is wrong on so many levels! What the hell is this guy securing!?!?"* Four hours later, when we began shooting my scene, I realized that the security guard outside my trailer, was in fact, the creator, producer and star of *Reno 911!* — Officer Dangle,

aka Thomas Lennon. He's also the creator and producer of the huge movie hit *A Night at the Museum, One & Two*. Looking back, I was grateful I kept all my comments and wisecracks about his wardrobe to myself.

A lesson that has stuck with me in this great profession of never knowing what to expect next. ◆

CAN I SHOW YOU A TRICK?

SENATOR CRANDALL

AS TOLD BY RON WILSON

Johnny Paul was a very fine close-up magician who owned a bar many years ago in Cicero, Illinois close to Chicago.

The bar was a favorite hangout for the mob. Johnny tended his own bar and hired Senator Crandall to do some close-up for customers in the evenings.

It was really late one night, and there was only one young guy with a girl sitting at a table.

Johnny said to Crandall, *"Can you go over there and show that couple a few tricks?"* With deck in hand, Crandall went over to the couple who were engaged in serious conversation.

He said something like, *"I'd like to show you a trick."* Without looking up at him, the guy quietly said, *"F**k OFF."* Then Crandall replied *"It's just a card trick."* Now the guy looked up at him and shouted, *"F*$#@&^*K OFF!"* Crandall mumbled, *"OK,"* and ambled back to the bar. Johnny then questions Crandall and asked, *"So how did you make out?"* Crandall replied, *"They want to see you!"* ♦

QUICK BITS

Dai Vernon told me this story about my old friend and fellow Scot **Johnny Ramsay**; a *get-together* in the mid-fifties in a Manhattan hotel. There were a few magicians sitting around in the afternoon. John stood up, took the watch out of his vest pocket and said, *"It's after 4 o'clock, time for tea."*

His right hand approached the left and he began winding up the watch, with the sound of a noisy watch winder. Everybody laughed. John slowly opened his right hand — no noisy watch winder, then he opened his left hand — no watch there either. Amazing.

— Ron Wilson

MAY THE FORCE BE WITH YOU

Jimmy Grippo

As Told by Ivan Amodei

NOT ANOTHER CARD TRICK!

Jimmy Grippo was a famous magician who worked as the house magician at Caesar's Palace in Las Vegas. But how he actually got the job there is as legendary as Jimmy.

He was performing for a few people at a small diner, when a friend of his brought over the general manager of Caesar's Palace in Las Vegas.

His friend told the manager (*let's call him Bill*) that he really needed to see Jimmy do magic because he wouldn't believe how amazing he was. Bill was not a big fan of the art and was not interested in seeing any magic at all.

Jimmy's friend said, *"Bill, if Jimmy really fools you, would you give him a job at Caesars doing magic?"* He said, *"Yeah, but he doesn't need to fool me, he needs to impress me, there's a difference."* Jimmy removed a deck of cards and began. Bill already knew it was going no where, but let him proceed. He has seen too many card tricks in the past and was unimpressed by most. Jimmy asked him to remove a card, look at it and place it back. So he did.

Then Jimmy spread the cards across the table and said, *"Bill, do you see your card in this deck anymore?"* Bill carefully looked and did not see his card. *"No,"* Bill replied. *"So what?"* Jimmy countered, *"Bill, where do you do your banking?"* Bill told him the bank name. Jimmy said, *"Now tomorrow, or the next time you go to your bank and go into your safe deposit box, you will find the card you selected there."*

Bill instantly began laughing at the notion of the scenario Jimmy just described. But he decided to play along and replied, *"If my card is there, I'll be back, and you will have yourself a job at Caesar's Palace."* Bill immediately left for the bank. When he was finally able to get into the vault, laying there on the floor was HIS selected playing card. He

18 Magic's Most Amazing Stories

was speechless. He quickly went back to the diner and told Jimmy he could have the job. ***So how did Jimmy do it?***

Jimmy was notorious for setting up things many days or even weeks in advance, and then patiently waiting for the perfect moment to strike. One day, while Jimmy was at his bank, he noticed the general manager of Caesar's Palace in line two or three people in front of him. He also noticed, he was going into the vault. Armed with a pack of cards, Jimmy decided to see if he could throw a card into the vault without anyone noticing. He made it. Now he just needed the amazing moment to arrive. If patience is virtue, Jimmy was its master. Some time later, when his friend approached him regarding Bill, Jimmy was locked and loaded

and ready to strike. Pure luck was on Jimmy's side that day. This was simple matter of taking advantage of a situation that could never happen again. I bet that today Bill still wonders how his card arrived in his bank vault only minutes after he selected it. Its simple: *May the Force be with You.*♦

Did you see it on CNN?
— ATTACK OVER ICELAND *page 45*

there's No key!
— CALL THE COPS *page 23*

God No!

— WHAT PARROT? *page 11*

WHEN I WENT THERE I REALIZED THAT THE AUDIENCE WAS COMPOSED OF PEOPLE BELONGING TO THE SUICIDE SUPPORTERS SURVIVORS GROUP
— YOU'RE KILLING ME *page 105*

I like to work alone!
— A SPLITTING HEADACHE *page 32*

My lawyer assures me everything would be okay
— A HOLE IN THE HEAD *page 197*

He found out they were going to give him $4000 to spend a few weeks studying with Dai Vernon
— BEATING THE ODDS *page 21*

the entire crowd stood and turned their backs on me
— ATTENTION! *page 29*

What possible use could a magician be to the war effort?
— CLEVER DISGUISE *page 91*

I was using very sharp scissors
— ME REHEARSE *page 35*

Wait a minute Jimmy, youse gotta take off yerse pajamas!
— ARE YOU KIDDING? *page 31*

BEATING THE ODDS

DOUG HENNING

As Told by Dennis Loomis

I n his last year at McMaster University, Doug called me from Toronto. He said he was going to apply for a grant from the Canada Arts Council.

They sponsored young artists for a full year to study in their field. But these grants were generally given to musicians, writers, sculptors, and painters–certainly not to magicians.

I was concerned that Doug was in for a big disappointment, so I cautioned him that he would probably not get the grant.

A few weeks later, he found out they were going to give him $4,000 to spend a year studying with Dai Vernon in Los Angeles, with Tony Slydini in New York, and also taking classes in acting, ballet, and other theatre arts. So much

> # THEY RAISED $40,000

for my concerns. While Doug was in Los Angeles studying with Vernon, the Arts Council funds were running low, so he moved in with another friend of mine, Jim Robertson. Jim has been most helpful providing dates and facts about Doug's early years to supplement my memories. After the year's study, Doug was required to stage a show to demonstrate what he had learned.

Again we spoke, and I asked Doug what kind of show he was going to do, where it would be done, etc.

He told me that he was working on a magic/rock musical with the assistance of Ivan Reitman, a friend of his from McMaster University. They planned for the show to run in December at the Royal Alexandra Theatre in Toronto. Again, I was afraid that Doug would

be disappointed. I told him not to get his hopes up, that the Royal Alexandra was the top legitimate theatre in all of Canada, and it was where you aspire to work at the end of your career, not the beginning. A little later Doug

and saw the show two or three times. They broke all attendance records for a short-run show at the Royal Alex! Ivan Reitman went on to Hollywood fame as the producer and/or director of *Animal House, Meatballs, Stripes,*

has made quite a name for himself as a composer of movie music, including the films The Aviator, Striptease, and the Lord of the Rings trilogy.

Spellbound had a lot of great magic, including Andre Kole's TABLE OF DEATH, Gene Anderson's TORN AND RESTORED NEWSPAPER, and Doug's very fast performance of METAMORPHOSIS. But my favorite was Doug's presentation of the FLOATING CANDLE performed with Jennifer Dale. Doug later did this for one of his television specials. ♦

TO STUDY WITH DAI VERNON

called to tell me that they had gotten the go-ahead, and their show, called *Spellbound*, would indeed be at the Royal Alexandra from December 26, 1973, to January 5, 1974. I went up for the opening, stayed for a few days,

Ghost Busters, Legal Eagles, and many more. Ivan and Doug had staged a preview show for potential backers of Spellbound and, amazingly, they raised $40,000. The music for Spellbound was composed by Howard Shore, who

This article/story originally appeared in the April 2009 issue of M-U-M, the magazine of the Society of American Magicians and it appears here by permission given to me by Dennis Loomis and Mike Close. Copyright 2009 by Dennis Loomis.

CALL THE COPS

IVAN AMODEI

As Told by Ivan Amodei

One night, I was working a gig at a private home and it was late. I had just finished up my show for everyone and placed everything back inside my bag and closed it.

I noticed a few teenagers were really anxious to get their hands into my bag and have a look around.

Nevertheless, I decided to go grab a bottle of water in the kitchen. When I returned, one teenager had actually opened my bag and was rummaging through it.

I said, *"Excuse me, but I don't think that is right you could just open my bag and look through it. What did you expect to find?"* He said, *"I'm sorry, but I thought all your stuff had gimmicks, and I could easily figure out your tricks if I got my hands on them."* I replied,

"Well, that's not the case." About 15 minutes later, I just finished talking with the gentleman who hired me, and I was about to leave. As I walked toward the front door, I noticed everyone at the party was gathered in a circle around the staircase.

I squeezed through the crowd to see what was going on. Well, the same teenager that was looking through my bag had actually stolen a prop from me. It was a set of *"legitimate"* police quality handcuffs that I used in my act earlier that night. He had taken them and hidden them away somewhere. I had no idea. He handcuffed his younger brother to the iron staircase of the house.

Hands through the other side and to each other. This young man was not going anywhere fast.

Here comes the big question of the day. His younger brother looked up at me and said, *"Well, can you get the key and get me out of here."* I replied, *"I don't have a key. They are just a prop and never to be used for real. I don't have a key."* He said, *"No really, stop being funny and get me out of these."*

THERE'S NO KEY!

NO REALLY, STOP BEING FUNNY AND GET ME OUT OF THESE.

I answered, *"No really, I'm serious, there's no key."* His parents then asked me what to do? I said, *"I think you are going to have to call the cops cause I think they are the only ones that have a universal key to get him out of these."*

They did call, but the cops said, *"Since it was not an emergency, we'll come some time later."* He had to wait until they arrived for freedom. He was locked into the handcuffs at 11:30pm on a Saturday night.

Before I left, this young man looked up at me and said, *"My brother will pay for this!"* I replied, *"I hear ya."* He said, *"Not because he handcuffed me to this railing, but because I gotta go to the bathroom really bad."* I laughed for about an hour straight.

That was punishment enough to be handcuffed there, but now add you have to really go to the bathroom and there is a house full of people. Holy S@#&^$! I stayed for another 10 minutes and since there was nothing I could do, I left.

I called the parents the next day and asked what happened. His mom said, *"The cops showed up, but not until 3:30am, and my son was sound asleep hanging from the railing. The cops said it was the funniest thing they've ever seen."* They said, *"How can he sleep like that?"* That kid was chained to his IRON staircase railing for four hours while his brother teased him the whole night.

I have a feeling that somehow over the next few months there was some sort of re-payment for what his older brother did to him.

I could only imagine.♦

SHE JUST APPEARED

ROCCO SILANO

AS TOLD BY ROCCO SILANO

Hank Moorehouse called me one day and asked me if I wanted to go on tour to promote the 2009 FISM (*The Federated International Society of Magicians*) convention happening in Beijing China. I agreed.

Briefly, FISM is the Olympics of Magic. Its only held every three years, in a European country and magicians from all over the world go to compete. One is crowned World Champion of Magic. FISM was held for one week at the end of July, beginning of August 2009. On this tour, I was performing with three other magicians and I was the closing act. Producers of the show asked me if I could do more than my regular 20-minute spot. They wanted me to do a one hour set. I asked, *"Why do I need to go that long?"* They said,

"We want you to go to FISM and do a one-man show and it needs to be one hour long." I was not thrilled about this request. First of all, I didn't want to add

more material to the show. Secondly, I didn't want to go to FISM. I had no interest in going at all. A 14–hour plane ride each way and all the headaches

that traveling that far comes with. No thanks! I was NOT going to FISM and there was nothing anybody could say or do that would change my mind. But I did

I'M NOT GOING TO FISM

agree to promote FISM, so I continued on. Late into the tour, I was backstage with one of my assistants, when I cut my finger pretty badly. I needed to be

ARE YOU KIDDING, OF COURSE I'LL BE THERE!

outside signing autographs right away. My finger would not stop bleeding. I was on a time crunch to get out there.

So instead of looking around for a band-aid, I just held my finger tightly and ran to the crowd.

From nowhere, I saw a person's arm reach across the crowd and hand me what looked like a tissue paper or napkin.

A soft voice then said, *"Here's something for your finger Rocco."* I looked up, and it was one of the most beautiful women I have ever seen in my life. Was I seeing things? She asked,

"Could I have your autograph?" I ran to my greenroom and told my assistant that I needed a photo right away and that there was the most beautiful woman I have ever seen in my life standing outside waiting for me to give her a signed photo. *"Come with me, you gotta come see her,"* I said.

I ran back outside to meet her again. Then she asked me, *"Rocco, are you coming back to China for FISM?"* Without thinking, I said, *"ABSOLUTELY, I'm coming back for FISM. Are you kidding, of course I'll be there. Wouldn't miss it for anything."*

Then she asked, *"Well, then could I be your assistant in the magic act?"* What do you think my answer was? YES!!! Nevertheless, I went to FISM and presented my one man show that turned out being one and a half hours long. Lots of fun. It was a great time for me and her. We were inseparable the entire time I was in China. I consider it to be the best time of my life.

And here's the best part. I asked her to marry me. She said, *"YES."* The moral to this romantic story is: **God works in mysterious ways.** And the story goes on happily ever after. ◆

Why is it called the Cup of Doom?

— CUP OF DOOM *page 179*

JNICEACKET!

JOHNNY PLATT

AS TOLD BY ALFONSO

O ne night my friend Johnny Platt worked out an elaborate publicity scheme. He knew that reporters hung out at this particular bar waiting for the latest scoop.

Johnny's most notable trick was vanishing a glass from under a newspaper. He placed a tall glass on the table. He then laid a sheet of newspaper on top of the glass and shaped the newspaper around it. He allowed everyone to feel the glass through the newspaper.

The newspaper was lifted to show the glass there one last time. After a moment, he placed his hand above the covered glass, and quickly slapped his hand down on top of it, smashing the newspaper flat onto the table. The glass was gone. It's a beautiful effect and

IT BROKE INTO A MILLION PIECES

was perfectly setup for this occasion, utilizing a newspaper as the appropriate prop for the journalists watching. But on this night, Johnny wanted to go the extra mile and have them **also** search him to prove the glass was indeed completely gone. As usual, Johnny placed the glass onto the table, covered it with a newspaper, and let everyone see and feel the glass.

As he returned the glass wrapped newspaper to the table, Johnny heard a loud crashing sound. Everyone saw glass shards scattered all over the floor.

What happened? Johnny didn't realize that his friend, acting as his accomplice, always bought his clothes from a *second-hand* store, and the jacket he had on had slits for pockets, but **no actual pockets.**

So when Johnny secretly slipped the glass into his friend's *"pocket,"* it fell through the slit, crashed onto the floor and broke into a million pieces.

Perhaps it was not the press Johnny was looking for, but it's a story we laughed at for many years. ♦

ATTENTION!

MATT MARCY

As Told by Matt Marcy

I was invited to do a show on a Naval Base to celebrate the retirement of one of the top officers. There were about 300 people in the audience and the show started off great. About midway through the performance, I got the guest of honor up on-stage and launched into one of my signature routines.

Everyone was laughing and having a good time until just before the climax of the routine, I heard a Bugle start playing off in the distance. For a brief moment, I thought nothing of it. Then, in unison, the entire crowd stood and turned their backs on me. Was it something I said? I stood there completely confused, and looked over at the Admiral on-stage with me. He explained that the Bugle signified it was time for the lowering of the base's flag — the colors — and it was customary to stand and face the direction of the flag from anywhere on the base.

About 60 seconds later the Bugle stopped. Everyone turned back and sat down as if nothing ever happened.

The momentum of the trick, of course, had completely ceased, so I just finished the end of the routine as quickly as possible and moved on. But I learned a valuable lesson.

If you perform on a military base and want to produce an elephant, all you need for misdirection is a recording of a bugle placed behind the audience. ◆

Tommy Cooper

QUICK BITS

Many years ago, I was an accountant and one of our clients was a large menswear shop in Shaftesbury Avenue, London.

Whilst visiting the client to do their annual accounts, I was regaled with the tale of how Tommy Cooper had been in recently to buy a suit. He tried the suit on and turned to the staff who were attending him and said, *"Do you mind if I take it for a walk around the block?"* *"Of course not, Mr Cooper,"* was the reply.

At which point, Tommy *magically* produced a small block of wood, placed it on the floor, walked around it and said, *"I'll buy it!"* Tommy left with suit and staff in stitches.

— Robert Agar-Hutton, UK

chapter
two

Naked people, crazy people, pranks, jokesters,
scissors, planes, terrorists, accidents, blind people

K ARE YOU IDDING?

JIMMY GRIPPO

AS TOLD BY JIMMY GRIPPO

One night there was a knock at my hotel room door in New York at about 4am, Jimmy relates. It was Rocky Graziano and about six other guys. Well, you know how Rocky used to mumble. Rocky said, *"Hey Jimmy, deeze hoodlums, dey don't believe youse can do it. I told dem how great youse are. Do some magic."*

I said, *"But Rock, it's 4 in the morning, what are you, crazy?"* *"Please,"* he said, *"I told dem youse could do it."*

So I started doing some tricks for them, but Rocky said, *"Wait a minute, Jimmy, youse gotta take off yer pajamas!"*

"Why?" I asked. *"Because dey figures if youse got clothes on you're hidin' somethin',"* he said. *"Youse gotta do it inna nude!"* So, as a favor for Rocky, I spent the next two hours doing card tricks in the nude. ♦

This story was originally published in the January/February 1987 issue of "Seven" magazine.

Did You Know?

Howard Thurston (July 20, 1869 — April 13, 1936) was a stage magician from Columbus, Ohio. When Harry Kellar retired in 1908, he handed over the mantle of America's Greatest Magician to Thurston. Today, Thurston is still famous for his work with playing cards and he was one of the first magicians to work with the back palm.

Thurston fooled Leon Hermann, nephew of Alexander Hermann (*another famous magician*) with his back palm. From that point on he called himself *"The man that fooled Hermann"* and used the publicity to get booked into top vaudeville houses in the United States and Europe, billing himself as the *"King of Cards."*

A SPLITTING
HEADACHE

JEFF HOBSON

As Told by Jeff Hobson

During my teens years, I fancied myself a manipulator and dove-worker. Didn't we all? Although I used an average of six doves in my act, I was never much of an animal lover.

Don't get me wrong, I took good care of my doves. They were fed, watered and cleaned, but I never took time to learn about the details of raising doves. This mistake led me to an unusual and embarrassing event at one performance at the Michigan State Fair of 1976.

All loaded up with my birds and ready to go, I stood *"backstage"* at a trade show booth for a locksmith company. It was a particularly hot day in August and with the absence of ample air-conditioning, the area where I awaited my introduction was humid and uncomfortable for not just me, but the doves as well.

Two of them sat patiently inside of my sleeves, one in each. Always one to be on time, I was prepared way too early.

The owner of the locksmith company wanted me to do the show in front of his booth. When the time seemed right and enough people gathered to make an audience, I would begin. As time went on, I became rather toasty, and I knew my feathered friends were as well.

A five-minute wait turned into over 25 minutes, as my *"loads"* were beginning to squirm. Oh yes, I checked on them every minute or two to be sure they had plenty of air, albeit warm.

Finally, the introduction came, and I entered the stage for my opening trick: FIRE TO DOVE. I held a lit candle in one hand and flash paper in the other. The hand holding the flash paper is also the same sleeve where my first dove is to be produced apparently from the flame. Having been in the *"moist"* environment in the past with this act, I knew there was a chance of the dove *"sticking"* inside my sleeve and not propelling out to my awaiting palm

---

MY FEATHERED FRIENDS WERE A BIT TOASTY!

I like to work alone.

as quickly as it should. I was worried, to say the least. The last thing I wanted was a burnt dove! I lit the flash paper. Blinding the audience for a split-second, while my arm dipped down and back up with just enough centrifugal force to eject the dove from the sleeve to my awaiting hand. NO, the dove did not stick. It appeared perfectly! Success, I thought! However, the audience at that time did not applaud like in the past at this great opening illusion.

They were captivated and watched as one egg was also *"produced"* and continued to fly into the audience only to break as it hit an audience member in the head! The dove laid an egg in my sleeve! It wasn't long after this performance where I decided to give up dove magic.

It is hard enough getting myself together for a show let alone six partners who have their own lives to lead. I like working alone.

And now the chances are much slimmer that I leave with egg on MY face! ♦

A CASE OF THE SHAKES

DON DRAKE

As Told by Don Drake

Because of a disability that I didn't know I had, I developed very bad tremors in my hands and arms. The way I found out about it is what makes it funny.

I am a very experienced magic pitchman, with some 20 years of selling magic decks of cards on the road. I was very successful and did this for so long, I thought the process had become quite automatic.

I was in the middle of one of my pitches, and may I say, without trying to build my ego, that when I pitch, I sort of lose myself in the pitch!

So here I was, working at the MGM Theme Park in Las Vegas, NV, when suddenly I realized that my hands were shaking rather badly. Without stopping the pitch for more those two seconds,

I simply shouted, *"Pardon my tremor, I'm from Los Angeles!"*

Suddenly the crowd started to laugh and I thought to myself, *"Don, that's a great line, write it down."* So I did, and now you've heard it as well. What really makes it funny is the fact that I had no intention of making it a joke. I was simply trying to let the audience know that I wasn't nervous.

I've used the line in every pitch I've ever done since then. ♦

Did You Know?

MAGICIANS OF ANTIQUITY

Magicians of ancient Egypt held some of the highest positions in the Royal Dynasty. Often being close advisors to the Pharaoh. In the Westcar Papyrus, a group of ancient scrolls dating back to the 12th dynasty lies in the Agyptisches Museum in Berlin. These relics reveal mystical tales of magicians and give us an insight into the importance of their place in the dynasty at the time.

ME
REHEARSE?

TOM OGDEN

AS TOLD BY TOM OGDEN

October 1976. I was on my second full season touring high schools around the country, so I was sure that I had experienced and coped with just about anything that could go wrong during an assembly program. Au contraire.

Late one night, ensconced as comfortably as possible in a cheaper-than-budget motel in the sparsely populated woodlands of the Idaho Panhandle, I had a brainstorm. I was already performing a cut-and-restored rope routine in my act. Wouldn't it be cool if I repeated the trick using a microphone cord? (*yes, this was in the Old Days, long before wireless microphones existed.*)

I had never seen anyone do the trick, but it was easy to plan out a whole routine in my head. I would pick up the cord with my left hand and secretly add a prepared, matching black loop as I retrieved the scissors from my table.

Fortunately, I had a FUNKEN RING with me, so I could make the cord seemingly *"spark"* as I cut it in two. I'd mouth a few words, pretending that the power had been cut off, and then, finally, I'd restore the cable.

All I had to do was find some extra microphone cord.

The next morning, I stopped in at a Radio Shack on my way to the high school where I'd be performing. I didn't want to buy a twenty-foot microphone cord. I wasn't sure if I'd like the bit enough to keep it in the act, and the cable was expensive. Instead, I bought a yard of TV antennae cord off a large spool.

Now, did I practice the trick before I performed it? Of course not. I knew the handling. What bad could happen?

The town in the high school was located was a few square blocks along the two-lane highway that trailed through the vast forestlands north of Boise. I was to perform on the gym floor, which was common for assemblies in that area. I was lucky that day: All of the kids were able to fit in the bleachers along one wall, so I could stand on

> I WAS LUCKY THAT DAY!

IS THERE A DOCTOR IN THE HOUSE?

center court facing in a single direction. (*Often, I'd have to do my act under one of the basketball nets and try to play to students sitting along both sides of the full length of the gym.*)

I had setup my own portable sound system that day, so I knew I had lots of extra cord to worth with.

As I prepared to go into the new routine, I doubled up a section of cable in my left hand, added the loop under guise of reaching for the scissors, copped the FUNKEN RING, and snipped. In the excitement of the performance, I had forgotten that, unlike rope, the antennae cable had a very thick metal wire running through it. I was using very sharp scissors, but even they were having a hard time cutting the cord in half. Finally, the cable gave way, but as the scissors snipped through, they slipped. In an instant, I had cut a quarter-inch V-shaped flap of skin into the side of my hand, almost down to the bone, right where my forefinger met the palm.

Blood squirted everywhere. Huge laughs. It happened so quickly that I don't remember having any pain, although I'm sure there was plenty. But I was acutely aware that I still had at least twenty more minutes left to the show. *"Is there a doctor in the house?"* I called out. (*Yes, I actually said it.*) Another huge laugh. By now, blood was dripping onto the gym floor. I reached into my prop case and pulled out a roll of gaffer tape. I quickly wrapped it around my hand three or four times until it looked like I had readied myself for a boxing match.

The pressure of the tape stopped the flow of blood, so it was back to the show. I somehow finished, including a straightjacket escape and a usually-dexterous LINKING RING routine.

After the show was over and the kids were filing out of the gym, the principal came up to thank me.

"I loved the show Tom, but you know, that bit where you cut your hand may have been a little strong for some of the kids." I assured him, *"I wasn't joking." "Look."* And I gave him a peek under

the duct tape. His face went white. I asked if they had a nurse. Well, no: That was a luxury in rural schools. Did they have a first-aid kit? We checked the football supplies in coach's office and found one butterfly bandage.

I removed the gaffer tape, washed my hand and gingerly pressed the Band-Aid into place. *"You know,"* the principal said, *"That hand probably should have some stitches, but the only doctor in the area is some guy who moved here from New York a few years ago. He's retired and lives up on the mountain, so he charges a fortune if he has to practice."*

The nearest hospital was in Spokane. I wouldn't be there till the following week, so with the bleeding stopped and a drugstore nearby to stock up on Band Aids, I figured I could soldier through the next few days. If the wound became infected, well, I could deal with that then. (*Ah, to be young and feel invulnerable again*). As it turned out, although my hand was sore for several weeks, it did eventually heal completely. But to this day, I carry a tiny white scar on my left index finger. It reminds me of the impetuousness of youth. And, that the show must go on. ♦

THE
JOKER

MAC KING

AS TOLD BY MAC KING

Years ago, when I was just starting out, I was performing in a comedy club in Knoxville, TN. A few hours before the Sunday night show, the owner of the club called me and told me he was bringing a woman to the show.

It was their first date and he wanted me to get this woman on-stage to participate in my show. Normally, I don't like to get friends on-stage. Their reactions are usually a little off. But he was the fellow who signed my check, so I agreed to do as he asked.

Later that night, when I got this woman on-stage, I was saddened to realize that she was the absolute wrong kind of person for the bit I was going to do with her. It's a pretty elaborate series of tricks, but part of it involves me

> # THE IS CALLED THE HOUDINI CHALLENGE NAKED ROPE ESCAPE

giving her a length of rope and stating (*as a joke*), *"This is called the Houdini Challenge Naked Rope Escape. I just want you to take off your clothes and tie me up."* This poor woman seemed like the meekest little mouse of a thing, and I was afraid if I told her to take off her clothes and tie me up, she might actually start crying. However, I had already committed myself to employing

her for this joke, so I went ahead with the bit. But when I told her to take off her clothes and tie me up ... **Boom she did it!** She yanked her dress off over her head and was standing there in only her panties.

There was the club owner, in the front row, snapping pictures of me and the **stripper** he'd hired as a joke on me! ♦

"We need Visas?"

— The Accidental Tourist *page 71*

HE WAS CRUSHED!

— The Plastic Coffin *page 41*

That's good, but that's not my card

— Class Dismissed *page 69*

Everyone must attend the show of the Great Houdini!

— Icy Escape *page 213*

Houdini would be proud — Trapped Underwater *page 143*

Bill, if Jimmy really fools you, would you give him a job at Caesars doing magic?

— May the Force Be With You *page 18*

I was just as surprised

— In a Jam *page 43*

People are going to blow up the plane!

— Attack Over Iceland *page 45*

I arrived early hoping that I would gain more details about who I was performing for

— Feel the Beat *page 205*

THE PLASTIC
COFFIN

JOSEPH BURRUS

AS TOLD BY IVAN AMODEI

Sixty four days from the Halloween that legendary magician Harry Houdini died, Joseph Burrus orchestrated a stunt that he hoped would put him on the map and make his idol Houdini proud.

HE WAS CRUSHED

The scene was set, and hundreds of spectators gathered to see Joseph Burrus perform BURIED ALIVE. Loud noise from the news vans wailed in the background as they began arriving.

Burrus' legs were bound in chains and his hands placed into regulation handcuffs. He was then laid into a small, clear Plexiglas coffin.

The dramatic clanking of the chains rang over a riveted audience as the coffin was lowered into a seven foot dark hole. Several men began to shovel over three feet of dirt on top of this small capsule.

A cement truck then laid 6000 pounds of wet concrete sealing the hole. Just over seven tons of material beat down on the delicate Plexiglas casket. It took ten minutes to completely fill the hole.

Silence fell. Just as last of the materials were laid, a sudden cracking sound echoed over the crowd. The immense pressure was just too much for the fragile plastic case to bear.

The wet cement and dirt instantly caved into the hole crushing Joseph alive. Most knew it was too late to get to him in time. Nevertheless, the crew frantically tried to rescue him, but their efforts were futile. Joseph had failed to correctly estimate the higher weight of wet concrete versus that of dry earth. Lack of planning cost Joseph his life.

In the audience were his wife and children who just witnessed the unimaginable. To those who believe that *"things"* always go as planned when attempting such extremely dangerous stunts, need to think again. ◆

Joseph Burrus (1958 – 1990)

CUT IT OUT

MATT MARCY

AS TOLD BY MATT MARCY

It was bleeding, of course, I didn't think much of it, assuming it was just a nick. But by the time my rope trick was over, it was clear that I was in need of medical attention.

But was I smart enough to stop the show? Of course not! So I asked a bar waitress to bring me some napkins. sticking together with blood. The audience, of course, thought it was part of the show, and laughed awkwardly as I struggled on-stage. At the end of the card trick, I knew I had to stop the show. I headed down to the ship's doctor who decided he had to cauterize the wound to stop the bleeding. Essentially, he used nurses couldn't stop laughing about the magician who cut off his thumb.

Once the wound was burned shut (*it took seven chemical sticks to stop the bleeding*), the doctor wrapped my now black thumb in about three inches thick of gauze. But the show must go on, right? An hour later I was back on-stage

IT TOOK SEVEN CHEMICAL STICKS

There were no band-aids in sight, so I held them awkwardly over my thumb as I launched into a card routine. Within seconds, the napkins had completely soaked through, and the cards were chemical sticks to burn the open wound shut. I highly recommend you avoid this procedure if ever possible.

Of course, while I was experiencing some of the worst pain of my life, the performing the second set of the night — gauze-wrapped thumb and all — for a very confused second audience.

Ever since then, I've considered rope tricks to be an occupational hazard. ♦

J IN A JAM

MIKE FINNEY

AS TOLD BY MIKE FINNEY

My greatest moment in magic, was while working at Magic Island in Newport Beach, CA. in the late 80s. I was in the big room doing the middle spot for Harry and Gay Blackstone. They would close with their floating light bulb piece.

I started doing my card on forehead routine. I had a large, Jumbo deck out and asked someone to take a card from it and said, *"Go ahead and place that card back into THIS deck."* Then I removed a regular-size deck of Bicycle Poker cards. Its absurd, but gets huge laugh every time. I then directed the spectator to stick the Jumbo card into the regular-sized deck.

The guy I selected, jammed the Jumbo card into the smaller deck *in-and-out* really fast. When he pulled the Jumbo

NEVER AGAIN FINNEY, NEVER AGAIN!

card back out, a regular-sized card split the seam of the Jumbo-sized card and they were both stuck together by their corners. He turned the card(s) over to look at them, and both the **Jumbo card** and the **normal card** were **identical**: a little Jack of Spades was stuck in the seam of the Jumbo Jack of Spades. I got an instant standing ovation. The audience went nuts.

What they didn't know was, it was a freak accident! I was JUST as surprised, but not going to say a word. The Magic Castle in Hollywood is the best place to see great magic. Apparently that day, it was in Newport Beach.

I looked over my shoulder and there were Harry and Gay wondering what the hell happened? Peeking through the curtains, they could see the audience standing and applauding for two to three minutes. Then I noticed Harry mouthing something to me, so I locked my eyes on his lips and unscrambled what he said, *"Never again Finney, never again!"*

What can I say? To have this happen while working with legends in magic was the best moment I've ever had in magic! I remember it like it was yesterday! ♦

ATTACK OVER
ICELAND

DAVID COX

AS TOLD BY DAVID COX

I was in Munich in the First Class Lounge, a scotch and a Leberkaese sandwich sitting nearby, while I waited four hours for my plane. Why? Because of the ATTACK OVER ICELAND! Do you remember that story of the Luthansa flight that had to ditch in Iceland because a passenger was attacked? Did you see it on CNN? I did! It was especially interesting to me, because I was that attacked passenger.

I was sitting next to this Polish guy, and he was drinking. A lot. I'm not saying anything about the Polish, I'm

> ## DID YOU SEE IT ON CNN?

just saying something about this guy. He was drinking a lot. He asked, *"Do djou haf wheesky?"* every time the stewardess came by. Eventually, as his words slurred more and more, they stopped serving him, and when they stop serving you liquor in Europe, you know someone is in trouble.

He seemed a little sad, and he looked at the stewardess with betrayal in his eyes, but I was sleepy, so I just drifted off. When the duty free cart came by, banging into my knee as it always seems to do, he sneakily bought a big bottle of Black Label scotch and drank it. All. I didn't know this at the time. No one did. They would have had a hard time IMAGINING it, and imagining that the guy would survive. They're required

to seal it in a big zip lock like bag, due to strict regulations, but the guy mumbled something about wanting to seal it himself because *"mumblemphfl,"* and the stewardess walked on. Germans. So sweet. So trusting. There were several dimly remembered instances of him talking to someone on a satellite phone and screaming at them in a variety of languages, and he got up four times to push past me to use the bathroom.

I was friendly, and moved, waking up each time, shifting my Harry Potter book and blanket, untangling the headphones, raising my tray table, getting up into the aisle, picking up my pillow, and then doing it all again when he came stumbling back to push past back into his seat, trailing his ass across me. Eventually, I offered to switch seats

I HAF NO FRENS

with him, you know, to make peeing easier on him. He said, *"No, because two months ago someone said 'NO' to me, and people are shit. So I say fucking no."* Then, when he came back, he said, *"I'm sorry. I am a piece of shit."* I told him, *"It's all right,"* and I went back to sleep. He continued to make vaguely threatening sounds, and had punched me awake a few times.

When I got up to use the bathroom myself, I asked the stewardess, in my most charming manner, to move me to another seat. ANY seat. Because I was getting very worried about the guy next to me, who was very drunk and increasingly violent. She told me that there were no other seats, and that the flight was completely sold out. She continued that I should return to my seat immediately. Later, I peeked into business class, which was almost deserted with PLENTY of seats. The stewardess seemed to feel that I needed to know my place and sit in coach. A bit later, my inebriated seat-mate yelled across me at a stewardess who was just trying to serve orange juice, which I thought was pretty nice of her. *"What do you fooking WHANT!?!?"* he yelled at her. The next thing I knew, he was punching me awake again. *"Why are hyou not my friend?"* I didn't know whether he meant why haven't I befriended him during the flight, or whether he was asking why I hadn't magically transformed into his childhood pal Yorge. In the end,

he told me he was going to kill me — and everyone on the plane — and that he was going to kick my fooking ass *"Keeeeek yur fooooooking ASS! Hoff! Dis! PLANE!!!!"* I summoned the juice stewardess back, and told her that we have a problem. She replied, *"We do have a problem, and that I was going to have to control my friend."*

I told her that he was NOT my friend, and this was apparently the wrong thing to say. He yelled, *"No! Not my friend! I HAF NO FRENS!"* Then he tried to punch the stewardess. I reacted with snakelike speed and slammed his hand into the seat back in front of me, preventing him from punching the juice girl in the face. We were both stunned at my action. He stared at his thwarted punching hand, and then, told me he was going to crush my face. He then hit me — a solid pop to the nose.

The fumes made me light headed

Then he grabbed my glasses and yelled something in Polish. He swung at the stewardess again. I grabbed his hitting arm, and two guys in the row behind me, grabbed his other arm, and we wrestled for a bit. I bopped his hand into the seat in front of me some more, which caused him to drop my glasses which he was apparently trying to stab the stewardess with. The guy in front leaned over and grabbed him. Things

Polish national on a German plane with an American book about wizards.

So I just held him. Soon, more attendants came up and asked me to step out. Finally, thinking that this way I could avoid international charges for book bopping, I tried to get up. He tried to hit a stewardess again — a different one — and I blocked him and grabbed his arm. He lurched forward and grabbed me in a hug, and said (*translated into*

up the plane!?!? I will! I will kill you all!" The fumes from his threatening maw made me light-headed. They had to be at least 150 proof. I stepped out.

They put me in a jump seat back in the galley, which was actually much more comfortable than my coach class seat. I discovered that I had blood dripping down the side of my head, and the purser just kept nodding at me like I'm five stating, in her pretty German accent,

PEOPLE ARE GOING TO BLOW UP THE PLANE!

had reached a stalemate. I had the Harry Potter book in my other hand, and I was thinking about bopping him in the nose with it. Hard. Then I thought about being the guy charged with assaulting a

non accented English), *"No! You are staying with me! We will know who you really are! We will know who we BOTH are! As PEOPLE! You are a liar! All of you are liars! People are going to blow*

"Everything is OK, yah? Hmm? Fine? Yah. You're OK. Yah? Mm-hmm? Yah. Yaaaaaaah." They offered me tea and a chocolate bar. It was good chocolate, and I felt a little better. Maybe I am five. Then the head stewardess went to sit down next to him to talk and calm him down. She was trained, and she carefully took off all of her jewelry and her little neckerchief before she sat down — which really impressed me. She stretched and limbered up, and then headed in. I'm sure that she was very reasonable and professional.

There was quiet for a bit. Then I heard him laughing. Cackling, and I thought, *"In no possible scenario can I imagine this as a good sign."* She came back to the back of the plane. She was now dishevelled and pissed.

She was talking very quietly in German. Scary quiet in German. It turned out that he had groped her, top and bottom, and squawked about it. So that's when they got out the restraints and decided to land in Iceland and kick him off the plane. A group of four big German guys held him down for over an hour while we diverted to a barren, possibly military field in Iceland.

All the while, he kept yelling, and going through all the stages of drunk ranting:

"I will kick your ass! All of you! All your ass!"

"Please! Please! I'm sorry! I don't mean it."

"George Bush! Fooking George Bush!"

"Please! I just want to go home! (weeping in Polish)" The pilot attempted to explain what happened and said, *"Ladies and gentlemen, we have an unruly passenger. We have asked him to calm himself, but he insists on being very disruptive. So we will be landing in Iceland, and putting this person off the plane. We apologize for the inconvenience."* Then he started in German, *"Mein herr and mein herren, blah blah blah unruly, blah blah blah Iceland, blah blah unruly, blah bitty blah."* Then, in French, *"Unruly unruly, pardon moi."* We landed in a barren field somewhere in the middle of Iceland. There is apparently nothing in the middle of Iceland. I looked out the window, and all I saw was ice, snow and a dirty white, all the

PLEASE, I WANT TO GO HOME!

Trains from now on

way to the horizon. We were seriously nowhere. Then some very BIG guys came aboard. They were all blonde, and had massive chests. Vikings. Clean us. That we were *s*%t*, that we were nobodies, and something more about George Bush. All in an accent that was at times, I'm sure, authentic, but mostly, human beings. Someone else said, *"Why? He didn't respect other human beings."* Now he's a Polish guy in jail in the middle of nowhere in Iceland

WHAT IS THE FINE?

shaven, crew cut Vikings. The drunk Polish man is still as drunk as he was two hours previously. He tried to tell them that he would kill them, but they said nothing, and just nodded to each other. Then they lifted him up in their arms, his feet high in the air, and carried him off the plane. He kept screaming about coming back and killing all of to me, comically Boris Badinoffy. He made a LOT of threats, but in the end, he was the one who was carried off like a carpet. A small boy from England, who thought the guy was *"bloody ludicrous,"* took his picture with a cell phone, hoisted high in the air, and was scolded by a French woman, who told him we needed to respect other for making terrorist threats, attacking an American passenger, and sexually assaulting the crew. He can't be happy. The 400 passengers are more than a little pissed off about a two-hour delay while we dealt with him. What's the fine? How much does it COST to divert a jumbo jet to Iceland? I don't know, but I bet that guy does. ♦

Where Are You?

BRUCE GOLD

As Told by Bruce Gold

I'll never forget the show I did at a retirement home when I was just starting out. During the vanishing bottle trick, I displayed an empty paper bag to an elderly woman in a wheelchair and asked, *"Do you see anything in there?"* *"No!"* She replied. The whole audience burst into laughter while I stood there, dumbfounded. After all, this wasn't normally a punch line. Finally, a nurse let me in on the joke and said, *"My dear, we're all laughing because she's blind!"*

Everyone laughed again, including me. It taught me that a genuinely spontaneously moment can be funnier than anything planned. I suggest you never try to stifle a laugh, even if it's at your own expense because it gives you a few extra seconds to think of what to say next. In my case, I asked the blind woman, *"From now on, please inspect all my props!"* ♦

QUICK BITS

Back in the Sixties, Francis Carlyle attended a lecture in New York City, in an old hotel with no air-conditioning.

It was very hot and humid, and the lecturer was really boring. One man got up, walked over to the window and opened it. Francis shouted out, *"Don't jump, it may get better!"*

— Ron Wilson

Magic's Most Amazing Stories   **51**

NOT IN A MILLION YEARS!

BEN JACKSON

As Told by Ben Jackson

College Station, Texas: embedded in the heart of Brazos County and home to the 48,000 *"Aggies"* of Texas A&M University. I was performing a formal close-up show inside my residence hall, Aston, for a mixed audience of students and dormitory staff.

close the night with my rendition of the INVISIBLE DECK, a mental miracle in which a spectator's freely thought-of-card is revealed to be the only face down card in a face-up deck. It is a solid effect that always plays big. Everything was going as planned, or so I thought.

After quickly scanning the crowd,

out of the imaginary pack of 52 playing cards you now hold 13 cards in your hand, the ace through king of clubs. Scan them over and focus on one. The rest of the cards are irrelevant. Do you have a card in mind?" He nodded. *"Great. For the first time in a loud clear voice, merely name the card you are*

A FLURRY OF CHILLS RACED UP MY SPINE

My closing effect became an unparalleled moment of my performing career. In short, the audience reactions rivalled a mob of David Blaine fanatics and the trick can never be repeated. I had it all planned out. I was going to

I asked a guy in the back of the room to assist me with the last trick. He came up, we exchanged pleasantries, and after a series of questions, he had narrowed down his selection to a club. I recapped the situation. *"Alright, so*

thinking of." He cleared his throat and announced, *"The Three. The Three of Clubs."* Suddenly a light bulb when off in my head! A flurry of chills raced up my spine. I remembered months earlier that semester, I had planted a *Three* of Clubs behind the very large glass wall behind where I was performing. Still in disbelief, of this strange set of coincidences, I made a glance over my right shoulder and there it was, tucked away in the corner. I had a miracle on my hands! I milked it for all it was worth and the line between confidence and arrogance had never been thinner.

Believe it or not, I had the audacity to ask him, *"Do you want to change your mind?"* What was I thinking? Thankfully, he was content with his selection. Tossing the INVISIBLE DECK away, I promptly modified my patter and said, *"Let's keep this strictly mental — no deck needed. Keep focused on the Three of Clubs."* The audience looked perplexed to say the least. Not even I knew how this was going to turn out.

However, I slowly walked toward the glass pane behind me, tapped on the surface verifying its solidity and turned around with a giant grin comparable to the Cheshire Cat. *"Solid piece of glass,"* I said. The audience let out an inaudible *"Duh. No one has been around this area, right?"* Shoulders shrugged with a slight nod of agreement which translated into, *"get to the point."* I pointed to the faint image of the *Three of Clubs*, which was barely illuminated by the surrounding light and exclaimed, *"Then this must be impossible!"* Insert pause of audience realization here. What followed was nothing short of barbaric yelps.

Screams of disbelief echoed through the hallways and there was nothing left to do but shut up, stand back, and the let the effect marinate like a freshly cut tenderloin. After the waves of shock and awe had subsided, the card was given to the spectator, and I wrapped up the show. Even though I was only on the third floor, I felt like I was on cloud nine. As I strolled back to my dorm, I was

DUDE, YOU'VE NEVER SHOWN THAT ONE TO ME!

Well, its a new one!

greeted by my roommate. Although he didn't attend the show, he was informed that the last trick was pretty incredible. Intrigued, I asked what he had heard.

Let me preface this by explaining a game I played in elementary school: **Telephone**. Briefly, there is a line of people (*roughly five or six*), and the person at the beginning of the line whispers a message to the next person and so on until it reaches the last person.

The last person then announces what he/she thinks the message is, and, without a doubt, it is always different than the original message. The intended few sentences become lost in translation, and sure enough my room mate fell victim to the role of the final message receiver.

He said, *"Well, apparently you brought someone up and asked them to think of a card, right?"* I nodded. *"Then you held the deck in your hand and the person named their card out loud."*

His tale proceeded to deviate from the truth. *"So then, with the deck in hand, you snapped your fingers and their thought-of-card levitated from the deck, was suspended in mid-air, and then propelled itself backward. It went through the glass and then stuck to the outside! Dude, you've never shown that one to me!"* I struggled to keep myself from breaking character and spilling the beans.

With all the seriousness that I could muster, I lied through my teeth, *"Well, it's a new one. It's the first time I've shown it."* And with that, the night ended with a coincidental phenomenon whose true story would become twisted to epic proportions: ***a funny story with an inconceivable ending***. ♦

chapter
three

London, out of control birds, school, traveling, miracles and things that could never happen unless you are a magician

Fred ordered his agent to "Book" the retirement village tour.

THE AUDITION

GEORGE SATERIAL

AS TOLD BY GEORGE SATERIAL

I received a call from a casting agent regarding an upcoming film shooting in the Boston area. The agent didn't have too many details about the scene, other than the leading characters would be watching a magic show while out on a date.

She asked if I was interested and suggested that I bring some magic to perform for the audition. I vividly imagined the scene a tall, dark, figure, dressed in classic tails producing white doves in some classy night club while the lead characters, seated at a candlelit table, engaged in romantic conversation. *"My silent dove act would be perfect!"* I thought. The next day, I packed the doves, grabbed my tux and set off to the audition. I arrived at the casting agent's office a little early so I could get ready

and warm up. I signed in, and submitted my headshot and résumé. Just for added insurance, I also submitted my dove act promo pictures. If you looked up *"magician"* in the dictionary, this is the photo you'd see. I was asked to have a seat and told that I would be called in shortly. In the meantime, I was given a script to look over.

While reading the script, I discovered the *"magician"* was actually a street performer, with very specific dialogue, working a crowd with his pet rabbit!

"I'm screwed!" I thought. I couldn't have been more miscast. The casting agent then entered the waiting area and asked me if I had any questions or needs. I explained what I had prepared, and that I usually performed this piece silently while music played in the background. She said not to worry, and to just say the lines while performing my magic. She then showed me where to change.

I was barely set when the agent came back and said, *"They're ready*

I COULDN'T BE MORE MISCAST.

for you now." I entered the audition room, introduced myself, and quickly explained what I had wanted to do,

THERE'S NO WAY I'M GETTING THIS PART.

and how I could adapt it to the scene. One of the panel members said, *"That's fine. Show us what you've got."* And so I began. Feeling overdressed and out of place, trying to remember my lines, shouting to an imaginary crowd, AND perform magic by producing doves. My timing was so thrown off, that steals I can easily do in my sleep became completely awkward and unnatural. I fumbled for every harness and lost all control over my doves. They flew away one by one, crisscrossing back and forth

around the room. One dove tried to land on a glass light fixture hanging on the wall, causing it to fall off and shatter on the floor. All I could do was stay in character and ad-lib. It had to be the worst performance of my life. When I finally finished the scene, the panel sat there without expression.

They began jotting down notes and shuffling papers. The agent said the typical, *"That was great, thank you for coming in, we'll be in touch"* line. Now, I still had to *"wrangle"* my doves! By this time, the birds were so spooked, they were extremely difficult to approach without them flying off

again. It felt like hours with everyone watching me chasing my birds around the room. In the meantime, the agent's assistant went off to find a broom to sweep up the broken glass fixture.

Once I had all the doves captured, I gathered the rest of my belongings, thanked them all for their time, and offered to help clean up the broken glass. The agent said that wouldn't be necessary, and thanked me once again for coming in. I quickly left the room. There was another performer getting ready to audition in the waiting area.

He asked me how it went, and wondered what all the noise was. I shook my head and said, *"Not good. There's no way I'm getting this part."* I wished him good luck and left. It was a long drive home. My wife asked me how it went. If I didn't laugh I would have cried as I explained the

whole experience. *"It's probably some small local film anyway,"* I figured. Thankfully, after about a week, the whole dreadful incident was behind me and out of my mind. About a week and a half later came *"the call."* I got the part! I was totally shocked. The casting agent suggested that since it was an outdoor shoot, it would be best to leave the doves at home and use a rabbit instead. Selecting the magic to perform was up to me. I was given a tentative shooting schedule, sent a revised script, and contacted by wardrobe. With two weeks to prepare, I was completely ready for the shoot when I arrived on set.

During the scene's setup, the director and assistant director approached me and asked what I would be doing. I went

THE FILMING WENT GREAT

through the blocking and suggested several ways I could perform the routine. At this time, the two lead actors also came up to discuss the scene as well. Once the scene was established, the assistant director stayed behind to prepare the shot. He turned to me, smiled and said, *"The director saw your audition tape and thought is was the funniest thing he's ever seen. He loved it."* All I could do was laugh in agreement. The filming went great! They gave me my own dressing room trailer to relax in and I felt like a star.

Months later, my wife and I were invited to the movie's premiere where we had a wonderful time and met quite a few celebrities.

Unfortunately, as is so often the case, my scene didn't make it into the film's final version.

As disappointing as that was, the whole experience was certainly one of the highlights of my career.

The film was *Good Will Hunting*, the director who *"loved"* my audition was Gus Van Sant, and the two lead actors I worked with were Matt Damon and Minnie Driver. ◆

FOG
LONDON

IVAN AMODEI

AS TOLD BY JENNIFER AMODEI

It was one of those perfect, gray, damp, London afternoons. A nice change from my sunny year round Southern California home.

Fifteen hours of travel left my mom and I frayed at the edges. With the last bit of energy, we extracted ourselves from the black taxi and heaved our luggage up the steps of the charming Inn we were staying at. Checked in at last, we collapsed on the squeaky, twin beds. *"Mom,"* I slapped her edge of the bed. *"Mom!"* I groaned. *"We have to stay up to get used to the time."* She gurgled, *"Your right!"* She sprung into action leaping from the bed, as if it were quick sand. Hair dishevelled and eye's rimmed in a crimson red. I muttered, *"Why don't we get out for a bit."* I wanted to find an antique magic book for Ivan. We made our way to the front desk. A distinguished, silver haired, Inn Keeper, hammered away at his computer. *"Cheers,"* he stated. His tone had a musical quality. My mom's American vernacular appeared tarnished against the posh English manner. Mom said, *"Yes, we would like to find rare books."*

Her voice was a bit brash. The effects of long travel. The Inn Keeper took note and continued plugging away at the computer. *"Really, really, rare books,"*

YES, WE WOULD LIKE TO FIND RARE BOOKS.

he inquired. Mom's face quickly turned panicked, as she interpreted, *"really, really, rare"* as meaning, *"really, really, expensive."* *"OH NO!"* she blurted out, *"More like a ...**medium** rare book."*

In perfectly dry, English humour and timing, the Inn Keeper stopped what he was doing, looked inquisitively at my exasperated mother, tilted his head and slowly lowered his tortoise-shell rimmed glasses with his index finger and said, *"SO ... you want ... A MEDIUM RARE BOOK right? Brilliant,"* he exclaimed.

With a mischievous smirk crossing his face. He reached out and handed us a small white piece of paper with the addresses of three local book stores he wrote down for us.

At the top of the page it read: Specializing in **Medium Rare Books.** We stumbled out into the rush of the city's sidewalk. Realizing the embarrassment of the situation combined with the affects of extreme jet lag, we bursted into uncontrollable laughter. That carried us all the way to the book store. It has been years since the trip to London, but to this day when I admire the lovely antique magic book on the shelf, I still laugh and think, *"Thank God it was only "**Medium Rare**."* ♦

Did You Know?

THE AMAZING DUNNINGER

Joseph Dunninger (Mentalist & Illusionist)
(April 28, 1892 — March 9, 1975)

He was a trailblazer and created amazing mentalism effects for television and was a pioneer for also performing mentalism on the radio.

He offered a reward of $10,000 to anyone who could prove that he was using *"stooges"* in his work. Sometimes he would even bump the reward up to $100,000. He boasted that he could reproduce any claim that a *"medium"* proposed was real. Dunninger said he could duplicate the identical scenario, but resort to magic techniques instead.

At the age of seventeen, he was invited to perform for Theodore Roosevelt and at the home of the famous inventor of the light bulb — Thomas A. Edison.

Then the cop did something outrageous.

He reached over and felt my arm muscle and

sneered, "You've got some pretty good guns there.

I bet you can take care of yourself just fine."

— THE PLANT *page 238*

Humbling a JERK

Richard Turner – The Cheat

As Told by Doug Gorman

Every magician has had a time in their career when he was heckled or harassed by someone. Richard Turner thrived on hecklers and was in a position to do what all of us dream of doing: put a jerk in his place. This particular night aboard a riverboat, a man called him over to his table. Let's refer to him as Mr. Jerk. He explained how he always won every time he played in Vegas. To hear him talk, he was a pro, and no one could beat him. He told Richard to sit down and play. As soon as the first sentence spewed from the man's mouth, Richard had the jerk pegged. The man was arrogant, bossy, and had to prove his superiority, even at the cost of the humiliation of those around him. Nevertheless, it was late, and Richard wanted to get upstairs and have his usual meal and came back

This particular night aboard the riverboat

HEY, WHAT'S THIS ALL ABOUT?

down when he was finished. Mr. Jerk said, *"Let's play some cards."* Richard said, *"You don't want to play cards with me. The conditions I can control are these: I will let you shuffle and cut the deck, name the game, and tell me which player you want to be the winner, and I can make it happen just as you call."* Mr. Jerk asserted, *"Not with me! "I always win!"* *He grabbed the deck from Richard's hands and told him*

to sit down, as he started thoroughly shuffling the pack. Richard said, "How many players do you want?" *"The four of us."* Mr. Jerk said, *"What game?"* Richard asked. *"Seven Card Stud,"* Mr. Jerk answered. Finally, Richard asked, *"And which player wins?"* Mr. Jerk snapped confidently. *"I will, of course,"* Richard was ready to deal when Mr. Jerk slammed his hand down hard on Richard's dealing hand and said,

"We're not playing for nothing!" He ordered each of his friends to pull out a twenty dollar bill and place it with his own twenty dollars. Richard reluctantly pulled a twenty from his pocket and placed it with the other three bills. Richard dealt around the table, making sure Mr. Jerk had the winning full house. Mr. Jerk grabbed the $80 and shoved it into his pocket and said, *"I told you I always win!"* *"Hold it!"* Richard said.

I'm looking for a friendly game of Poker?

"It was no coincidence. I told you that you could name the number of players, the game, and the winner, and I would began winning hand after hand causing Mr. Jerk to break many one hundred dollar bills. Richard walked away with *been rude to everyone in this place. He thinks he's somebody, but you showed him he's not!"* Richard was later called

THE MAN WAS ARROGANT

make it happen." Mr. Jerk said, *"What are you talking about?" "I am the one that said four players, called the game, and said I was going to be the winner!" "Okay,"* Richard said, *"Get your money back out, and let's play again."* Richard an inch thick stack of $20s. During the game, the manager was standing about ten feet behind Richard smiling as he watched him clean out Mr. Jerk. As Richard showed his wad of cash, Joe said, *"That was great! That man has* back down. Someone wanted to see him. Guess who? It was Mr. Jerk who wanted to play one more game. He told Richard to sit down, and he was going to make sure every card came off the top of the deck and that the deck was

GET YOUR MONEY BACK OUT AND LET'S PLAY AGAIN.

thoroughly shuffled. He grabbed the deck and shuffled it 14 times before he handed it back to Richard. Richard was over-animated as he dealt the cards and said, *"Watch very closely! Are you watching?"* Mr. Jerk still missed it, as Richard dealt from wherever he chose. He took the four twenties and said, *"Thanks for a pleasant evening. Next time you make your friends play, know who you're challenging."* The waitress that had been catering to Mr. Jerk all evening came up to Richard and told him how the man wanted to know who he was. *"I told him you are the best cheater in the country, and that he was stupid to have challenged you. That's why he wanted you to come back and

play again. He thought he could catch you. Thanks for taking care of him for me."

Richard handed the waitress the winnings form his last game and said, *"Have a meal compliments of Mr. Jerk."*

For those of you who do not know, Richard Turner has vision four times **lower** than what is considered legally blind.

Most of the time, he cannot see the cards that are directly in front of him, and relies a great deal on his touch and feel around the deck.

He is an inspiration to our field and proof that anyone can accomplish anything they set their mind too. ♦

Did You Know?

JOHN GARDNER

The author of the 14 most recent James Bond thrillers is a magician.

John Gardner, retained by the estate of Ian Fleming, the creator of the Bond character, was a professional magician before he became an author.

One of his novels, *The Confessor*, is a thriller about a master spy who is also a secret master magician.

You're Italian, I can sense it
— THANK YOU MAESTRO *page 194*

I need 144 condoms

— BETTER SAFE THAN SORRY *page 249*

EVERYONE WAS EXTREMELY FRIENDLY EXCEPT FOR ONE GUY WHO WAS TRYING TO FIGURE EVERYTHING OUT!
— CLASSED DISMISSED *page 69*

Make it difficult for me
— I NEVER MISS *page 241*

Can you do that trick where you stick the half dollar to your forehead
— A HOLE IN THE HEAD *page 197*

I decided to go back to the airport because I thought maybe I could get some answers in person
— UNDER YOUR NOSE *page 185*

We had to evacuate the entire building

One January 17th, 1904, The President of the United States, Theodore Roosevelt took his children, daughter Ethel and his three sons, Archie, Kermit and Quentin to the Lafayette Theater to see Kellar perform.

— GOING OUT WITH A BANG *page 103*

— GUINEA PIG *page 129*

CLASS DISMISSED

RICK MERRILL

As Told by Rick Merrill

There is always one in the crowd. A person that is a bit more out spoken then the rest and always trying to figure out how everything worked.

One night around a table of six, there was to the right of me a man that was a perfect example of this. With my years of experience, I anticipated the situation and before launching into my full act. I setup the finally trick by placing a card under his drink. Then had him pick a card. Everyone at the table was fixated on the two of us because we had been exchanging friendly banter as the routine progressed. I turned to him to find his card. I explained that we would spell down to his card, removing one card from the top of the deck for each letter in the name of his card. When we were finished spelling, his card would be the very next card. I knew this wasn't going to work because his card was already under the drink, but I wanted to make him think that I messed up. I led him down the garden path.

I asked him the name of his card and he promptly replied, *"the King of Hearts."* So I started counting down from the top of the deck, putting one card on the table for each letter. When I reached the last *"S"* in Hearts, I turned over the next card and there, staring up at me was the King of Hearts. At that moment, I think I was the only one surprised by the what happened.

Everyone at the table started clapping because somehow, I had done what I said I was going to do. They all thought the trick was over until Mr. Vocal chimed in and said, *"That's pretty good. But that's not really my card."* Up until

THAT'S GOOD, BUT THAT'S NOT MY CARD.

that moment, I thought I had screwed up. I thought I must have palmed off the wrong card under his drink. As soon as he said, *"That's not really my card,"* I knew I had him. Just think of what must have been going through this guy's head. He tried to throw me off. So when I told him I'm going to spell to his card, he named some other card and then I actually spell to the card he named.

What are the chances of that? However, he thinks he's still the winner because I haven't found his card. He thinks he threw me off thus his comment *"That's pretty good. But that's not really my card."*

I'm not cocky or arrogant by nature, but the friendly sparring we participated in earlier made me realize I could push the envelope a little bit with this guy.

So when I said in my best parent scolding his kid tone, *"That's because your real card is under your drink. Never screw with Mr. Magic."* All of a sudden, Mr. Vocal became Mr. Speechless. He lifted his drink, glanced around the table at everyone looking at him, and then slouched back into his chair, throwing his *"real"* card face-up on the table. He was defeated. Class dismissed. ◆

QUICK BITS

When I first came to the United States, I was doing close-up magic on one of those dinner cruise barges on the Erie Canal in Upstate, New York.

There was a group of teenage girls in the corner and they came up to me and said, *"Are you a magician?"*

I said, *"Yes."* I spoke a little more and they said, *"Oooh, you're from England aren't you? We love the way you talk."*

I said, *"Yes."* One young girl about eighteen years old asked me, *"Can I ask you a question please?"* I said, *"Go ahead."*

She said, *"Did you learn English **before** you came here?"*

This was my *"Welcome to America!"* Two countries divided by a common language!

— Rachel Colombini

THE ACCIDENTAL
TOURIST

JASON LATIMER

AS TOLD BY JASON LATIMER

It was my first time traveling to India and hopefully my last. I was quite honored to be invited amongst renowned scientists from around the world. The students of the university put on the event doing everything from booking the performances to the lectures and workshops.

We had been discussing the show for months. The show, the extra equipment needed, extra plane tickets, oversized luggage, and even vaccinations. I was pretty sure we had covered it all.

In fact, I knew this was going to be such an amazing experience, we brought on an extra set of hands just to help document everything on cameras because we never wanted to forget it. Well everything that could have gone wrong DID, and there is no way I'll ever forget that trip. I know because I tried. We arrived 6am at Los Angeles International Airport (LAX) for a 9am flight to quickly find out we are not able to board the flight because we did not have visas. *"We need visas?"* I thought to myself, and realized that my management, and every email I could bring up on my phone, never once mentioned a visas at all. That's right, we need a visa. No way on the plane without it.

How did that get overlooked? I began madly trying to get a hold of our contact in India at whatever time it was for him, while another one in our group was trying to find out the fastest way to get visas for India. I reached my contact

WE NEED VISAS?

on the phone and said, *"You never said anything about visas."* His response to that was, *"Well, we sent you an invitation for you come to India."*

I replied, *"Yeah, but you never said we want you to come to India, now go use this email to get a visa."*

We eventually came to realize that all we needed to do was go to the Indian Consulate in Los Angeles and get our visas approved on a same day visa application. Sounds easy right? Wrong.

We found out that the Indian Consulate in Los Angeles does not approve the visas in Los Angeles. They send the passports and information by mail up to San Francisco, CA to get approved and then mailed them back.

However, we were told that if we could get our passports into the San Francisco Indian Consulate by 5pm today or at least 9am tomorrow we could have them ready by 5pm tomorrow and be back on our way. Looking at my two stagehands and a cameraman staring back at me with a camera in my face, I decide there's only one thing to do. *"Guys,"* I said, *"We are going to San Francisco."* I immediately got on the phone and purchased four first available tickets to San Francisco, while waiting in line to check in.

I reached the front desk and the tickets were not ready. Apparently, there is a security/time check between last minute flights and boarding, unless you want to pay an additional $20 per ticket for purchasing them at the front desk. Since I already bought them while waiting in line, I asked what we should do since our flight was about to leave.

The kind lady at the desk suggested that if I didn't mind the extra fee I could re-buy the tickets and my credit card company should see the double purchase and reverse the first purchases. Since I had no time to wait, I put my faith in the credit card gods, and the professional suggestion of the kind lady, and bought the tickets again.

We laughed it off, and made it on the plane to enjoy an early, yet much needed, cocktail as we explained the situation to the flight attendants and surrounding passengers. What I didn't know was that while I was in the plane, and my phone was off, my credit card

We are going to San Fran

company did see the eight tickets being bought in five minutes, but couldn't reach me so they shut off my accounts.

We arrived. We had to rent an SUV because we brought the gear for the show with us on the plane, and I quickly found out that my accounts had been shut off. I got those turned back on, which was the easiest part of the trip. We raced out of the airport. We went as fast as four guys and six pieces of luggage two of which were over sized could go. While laughing, because its all being caught on film.

We arrived at the consulate to find we had none of the things we needed, namely photos for the visas, cash, or even a check. We literally ran down

I think they're open til 6am

the street to get them and came back. We madly filled out the forms for the application as the clock was ticking closer and closer to 5pm. I handed all the paper work in, and heard these words, *"Great, it looks like everyone is perfect except this guy,"* as the official at the consulate holds up MY passport. What? It turns out that the visa needs four squares of the passport, all congruently next to each other to make up one larger square. I don't have that.

I have been traveling so much that even though I have space for a few more stops, I don't have four on the same page. It was 5pm and the official

IT HAPPENS TO EVERYONE

told me, *"Look, it happens to everyone. There is a U.S. passport agency down the street and they should be able to add pages into your passport without a problem. If you run down the street a few blocks they are right there. I think they are open till 6pm."* I looked around at everyone and realized I was the only one that was actually going to run the whole way there and quickly said, *"I gotta go."* I ran and got there sweaty and out of breath, only to find out they closed at 4pm. But there's a number to call! *"I'm saved,"* I thought. I called and found out that they are by appointment only and that there were

no open appointments available for a week. They open at 8am, but I didn't have an appointment. I was just going to have to make it work, because I had no other option.

We got a couple of hotel rooms, and by this time everyone was beat and dead tired from literally running around town. Meanwhile, I personally sweated it out that night, hoping to plead my case the next morning and sneak in an unscheduled appointment.

I woke up at 6am, took a few deep breaths, drank lots of coffee, looked at the e-mail on the phone, and decided to sit in front of the building from 7am to 8am just to see if I could speak to someone. It worked! They let me in without an appointment.

I got to the front desk of the agency to explain, and they told me it would take days to get pages put into my passport, or at least hours when rushed. I explained how I got here, and they decided that they wanted to help me. I waited 40 minutes until a little old lady came out from behind the security desk with a small box of tools to insert the pages. She added pages into my passport literally in the hallway of the waiting area. I don't know if that's standard, and I don't know if the $65 in cash was the real cost, but to be honest, at this point I didn't care.

By this time it was 8:50am, and I had to be down the street at the Indian Consulate by 9am in the middle of downtown morning San Francisco traffic. With my passport in hand, I grabbed the cameraman with his gear and literally threw him into the SUV as we took a few, how should I put it best, not the most legal turns and routes, as we tore through the downtown streets

of San Francisco like a car chase in a movie. I got there and ran in. I threw the passport onto the desk of the Indian

DON'T WORRY, THEY'LL BE READY BY FIVE

Consulate at 9:06am, and the lady official smiled and said, *"I was wondering if you would make it."* I replied, *"Sorry, I had a few traffic laws in my way, but I did the best I could,"* *"Don't worry,"* she said, *"They'll be ready by 5pm."* I looked back at the cameraman and his first response was, *"Wow! That was awesome! Jason, would you mind going back to get a few close-ups of those one way street signs?"* We got our visas that evening, and we flew back to LAX the following morning. We jumped on our

new flights to India, thinking now our trip could begin. After all the hassles, after all the last minute arrangements, after all the comments about our gear and our tickets to our contact in India, we were greeted in India with a warm welcome and much appreciation that we went through and what we did to get there.

However, I looked out to see that our greeter had brought a taxi about the same size as an old English taxi. I'm talking about the ones that barely seat four, except we had four adults plus six pieces of luggage, two of which were 4′ by 2½′ by 1′. I still have no idea, to this day, how the greeter was planning on getting to the university with us. Maybe the roof? Without even really asking, the locals, about 12 of them, in an effort to earn tips, began picking up the gear and loading it into the taxi. Of course the gear, as expected, took up 90% of the little car. Seeing this, the greeter turned to me and said, *"I don't think we are going to fit."* I looked at him, smiled and replied, *"Reeeeeally?"*

Our greeter suggested an idea. We separate from the gear and go in a different car. We have another car pick up the equipment, because he didn't have enough money to cover two taxis at the same time for such a long trip. I said, as politely as I could, that wasn't going to happen. The whole scene was becoming very suspicious about separating us from our luggage. Maybe it was a culture/translation error, but it

seemed so weird I quickly told Tom, one of my stagehands, to just jump in the front seat of the taxi with the props. I needed him to hang out with the driver that spoke no English till we could figure something out.

Over the next half-hour we were trying to figure out the transportation issue with phone calls, text messages, and email with the greeter's boss. Eventually we arranged for them to

---

I DON'T THINK WE ARE GOING TO FIT

---

send an SUV with racks on top. It would take an extra hour, but they would be able to take all of us at the same time. Good. My stagehand, and even the cameraman looked happy, but

we were missing something. *"Oh my God, Tom!"* I thought. I looked up to find the taxi that Tom was in no longer there. I was then told by laughing locals that since the taxi was blocking traffic, Tom and this *non-English* speaking cab driver had been circling the airport for the last 30 minutes, and Tom had been waving to us in the background of the camera shots as he passed by each time.

It then became an ongoing joke, as he continued to pass us by, we waved to him to said, *"Hi"* and *"Bye."* We made it after a few hours to a very excited campus of students with literally thousands of people eager to see the magic show. Rehearsal was pretty entertaining for me. I spent at least an hour working with a guy going through each sound cue with broken English until we had it down perfectly. Of course, after the hour or so of practicing with him, another student came in to ask if he should learn these cues because the guy I was talking to wasn't a member of either the stage crew nor sound crew. He was just a random guy that was hanging out in the theater and he didn't know how to say he wasn't the sound guy, so he went along with me to be polite.

Now my guys are pretty electronically proficient. My stagehands are all composed of engineers, so it was pretty funny to me when I asked for one of my guys to turn off a light by unplugging it, and heard his response, *"Are you kidding me? There is no way I am touching that."* With a couple of deep breaths, we made

it work. We had no choice, the show had to go on. The time came for the coordinator and myself to work out the business aspect of the shows and exchange receipts and fees. However, when it came time for payment, he approached me and said, *"I am very sorry, but we couldn't locate enough American dollars to pay your fees, so we collected the amount in Indian Rupees (INR)."* (47.8 INR to $1 USD) It turned out the largest bill for the Indian Rupee is a $500 bill, which came out to being $10.45USD.

I was collecting a fee that was enough to support my show, a group of four, shipping, travel expenses for the week, a quick stop in San Francisco, and compensation for our time of traveling

> I WAS BEING SIZED UP

half-way around the world in cash. He then pulled out a backpack full of Rupees and handed it to me right in front of their stage crew, my stage crew, and random people cleaning up the theater. It was literally just a bag of cash.

The average individual in India makes about 150NRI a day, about $3.00USD, and when they said the word *"cash"* and held up the bag, it felt like it echoed in the theater to the point that my hair started to stand up on end without all the gel I normally use.

I quickly felt I was being *"sized up"* by everyone in the theater, so I grabbed two of my stagehands and told them we had to go to the hotel immediately. We raced out of the theater in the middle of

This is insane

rehearsal. Outside of the campus theater we found a few students we had met earlier, each with their own Vespa motor scooter. I gave them each a 100 Rupees, and we all hopped on the back of the bikes and tore off to the hotel. Racing through a remote campus in India on dirt roads with a backpack full of cash on the back of a motor scooter of a random man whom I had just met only a few hours before. Oh, the glamorous life of a magician.

We ran up to the room and emptied the backpack on to the bed. We then filled our pockets and clothing with all the cash and walked back to the theater to give everyone the impression the money was in the room.

We then placed all of the cash in our prop on-stage because we knew it would be in our sights the entire time. In the end, our group had an awesome show and the university had a great time.

We eventually made it back to the old airport, and I boarded the Air India flight, sat down, and took a deep breath. I was so happy to be on the plane. It was an old plane, but it was still a plane. I was going home and I survived. Right then, for some reason, a part of my seat fell off in my hands.

The flight attendant ran over with a Tupperware container of used nuts and bolts that looked like she had accumulated it from ones found laying around the plane over the years.

She quickly put the seat back together like she did this every day. *"This is absolutely what I need right now, let me tell ya,"* I thought to myself.

Of course we all made it home safely, but not without a few more scares along the way. When I got home, I found the adventure had a twist.

The India Rupee is not a currency of exchange in the United States. One has to locate a special broker a steeper exchange rate to exchange the backpack full of Rupees to Dollars, but after making it home safely, I didn't care. Actually, the fact that the United States banking system didn't accept Rupees felt about right after all that.

There was nothing to do but laugh. I was sitting at home, for about a week, trying to figure out what had happened on that single trip and how it was actually all on film, when I got a call.

It was my agent. *"Jason, its Dennis. The Indian Institute of Technology New Delhi called, they caught your show in Kharagpur. They had a blast, and they want to know if you are available in a few months. What do you think?"* ♦

HEATING PROBLEMS

ALDO COLOMBINI

AS TOLD BY ALDO COLOMBINI

In Italy, I was invited to a show in a town called Udine. I was living in Maranello, about four hours by car from there. It was cold in Italy during the month of December. We have some good cold winters.

My great friend Angelo said that he wanted to go with me to my show. I told him that the heater in my car was broken, so it could be a bit cold in the car. He said, *"Don't worry about it."*

And we're on our way. We were having fun talking and shooting the breeze, when I noticed that about an hour into the trip, Angelo completely stopped talking to me.

Actually, I didn't realize how long he was not talking to me until I thought about it. At least a full 30-minutes of saying absolutely nothing to me. I glanced over at him and he was tightly huddled up into a ball. You see the freezing cold air was slipping in from the front of my car and coming up through his side. I was completely fine. After all, I knew how

DON'T WORRY ABOUT IT!

HEATING PROBLEMS

to prepare for my trip. I had blankets and extra layers of clothes on to keep warm.

But not Angelo. Can't say I didn't warn him. Freezing cold air was sweeping up and over his legs, across his chest and onto his face for over 30 minutes solid. He was literally frozen.

I gazed over at him and said, *"Are you okay?"* He slowly turned his head toward me (*I think his neck was thawing out*), and with a straight face said, *"Would you mind pulling over so I can get out and warm up!"*

I could not stop laughing. It was the funniest thing I had ever heard, plus the look on his face, the position he was in and the complete package made it something hysterically funny.

As as side note, Angelo never accompanied me on any more trips. ◆

MICHAEL SKINNER

Mike was the house magician for 20 years at the Golden Nugget Hotel and Casino in Las Vegas and he had many repeat appearances on *The Tonight Show* with Johnny Carson.

Anyone who visited him at the Golden Nugget at the Lillie Langry Restaurant, got an *eye-opening* look into the art of magic and Mike's masterful approach to this wonderful art.

He was also famous for his extensive repertoire. One time, while performing at The Magic Castle in Hollywood California, Mike performed 28 straight shows and ***never*** repeated a single effect. Amazing!

then I noticed that he completely stopped talking to me. Actually, I didn't realize how long he was not talking to me until I thought about it. At least a full 30 minutes of saying absolutely nothing to me. — HEATING PROBLEMS *page 79*

Yes, the elephant did vanish, but

— A BIG SURPRISE *page 245*

SAY CHEESE

RICK MERRILL

AS TOLD BY RICK MERRILL

Real Magic. It's something every magician hopes will happen. That unexplainable mystical moment. It happened to me one night during a gig. I was performing a coin routine for a table of two when I sensed something to my right.

I turned to see what had caught my eye. I looked down to see a 5 year old girl holding a camera. She wanted to come over and take a picture of the magician. The girl asked if she could take my picture. I looked back to the table I was performing for, and they were smiling at how cute the little girl was. It was obvious they wouldn't mind if I had my picture taken. I turned and faced the little girl and she held the camera up to her face and snapped my picture. The flash went off, which attracted the attention of even more tables in the restaurant. The little girl smiled and said, *"Thank You."*

Before she could leave, I grabbed my deck of cards off the table and asked her, *"Would it be OK if I took her picture too."* She said, *"Yes,"* and started to

IT WAS ONE OF THOSE RARE MOMENTS

hand me her camera. I told her that I didn't need to use her camera because I had my deck of cards. I held the deck of cards up to my face like a camera and asked her to say, *"Cheese."*

As she did, a bright flash went off from the deck of cards and I heard audible gasps from many people in the restaurant.

The little girl's eyes got very wide as she started to register what had just happened. I told the little girl, *"Thanks for the picture,"* and that I would hold on to it for a long time. With eyes still wide in wonder, she turned to look at her parents for direction.

I'm convinced that the little girl, her parents, the people at the table, and the entire restaurant still remember that moment and believe that is was real magic. ♦

Did You Know?

Alexander Hermann was born in 1843 and is one of the biggest names in magic. Even today, his name and reputation are revered by many prominent magicians.

He worked extensively in the U.S. and Europe and became famous for his large scale illusions. One illusion CREMATION which involved burning his wife Adelaide alive was a centerpiece of his show. After the burning, ghosts hovered over her coffin and around the stage to the audience's shock.

Hermann also performed the dangerous *BULLET CATCH*. Alexander's version though, magnified the original presentation by having ***five or more*** guns loaded, aimed and fired at him. He caught all the bullets with the help of a china plate. He died on December 17, 1896 (*age 53*) and received the most extensive newspaper coverage & publicity for a deceased magician to date.

chapter
Four

Houdini, trees, pranks, glue, hypnosis, police cars,
The Magic Castle, Islands and more

Lock PICKING

Harry Houdini

As Told by Avani Mehta

Unquestionably, Harry Houdini is the most famous escape artist in the history of magic. I'm not sure if the story I'm about to share with you is part of his legend or part of his history, but it surely is fascinating.

Houdini was very confident in his talents. He claimed that he could escape from any jail cell in the world in less than an hour, provided he could go into the cell dressed in street clothes.

And every time he was given this challenge, he accepted and did just as he promised. Being left alone in a locked cell, and in just a few short minutes, he would miraculously escape. But one time things didn't go as Houdini planned. A small town in the British Isles built a NEW jail cell and they were proud of it. *"Come give us a try,"*

HOUDINI LITERALLY COLLAPSED

they said to Houdini, and he agreed. He walked into the prison cell bristling with confidence. After all, he had done this hundreds of times before.

Inside his belt, Houdini hid a special lock pick he designed. Once the jail cell was closed, he took off his coat, and set to work with his special lock pick. But this time, he discovered that something was unusual about *this* particular lock.

For 30-minutes, he worked and got nowhere. And his confident expression disappeared. An hour passed, and still he had not been able to open the door. By now, he was bathed in sweat and

panting in exasperation, but he still could not pick the lock open. He tried all the tricks of his trade, everything in his arsenal, but nothing worked.

After two hours and totally exhausted, Houdini literally collapsed against the door. Surprisingly, the door swung open. Houdini discovered, it was NEVER locked in the first place! He never bothered to check. It was locked only to him in his mind. The lesson. Never assume. Anything is possible. ♦

HIGH NOON

SHAWN FARQUHAR

AS TOLD BY SHAWN FARQUHAR

To be honest, I don't usually get up before noon. But I got up for this call. It was an agent from Notable Entertainment. Unfortunately the gig was not that attractive. A luncheon, and given my nocturnal schedule, I was not thrilled. However, I was at the time honing my act for a big competition so I took the job.

Upon arrival, the president and organizer of the luncheon informed me I needed to do *two sets* of thirty minutes and not a one-hour show as indicated on the contract. I tried to explain that I had just brought one opening effect and a single closing effect, and that the show would not be as well received if I were to alter what I had planned for their group.

They, on the other hand, were adamant that I do *two sets* as they had a special presentation to conduct between my acts. After much discussion, they told me that if I could not abide by

I HAD JUST DRIVEN FIVE HOURS

their wishes, my services would not be required. I had just driven five hours and was not looking forward to driving home without some money in my pocket for my effort, let alone the loss of sleep!

I agreed to the two thirty-minute spots and began to set the stage. It was a standard ballroom pipe and drape riser,

but it had an easel on the back center of the stage with a large picture covered by an even larger dark cloth. I asked if it could be moved, and they replied it was needed for the special presentation and

that it had to remain.

It was an eclectic gathering of the local business people, and they were seated and fed rather quickly. To my surprise, the president introduced me on time and I started the show I would never forget. The first thirty minutes were fabulous, and the audience responded to the jokes and magic quite well. I would like to say, I thought something was amiss, but to me, all was well. I ended the first half of the program with an effect that was not as strong as I would have in the service corridor. As I walked back towards the backstage area, I saw a worried look on wife's face. I asked her what was wrong? She told me I had to see for myself. I peeked through the pipe and sobbing. The two young people next to her were just as traumatized by whatever was taking place at this special presentation. From where I was watching it was hard to see or hear, so I made my way to the other end of the banquet hall. From my new vantage point, I could see a painting of a park with children and families playing beneath three large

I WAS STUNNED. WHAT DO I DO NOW?

liked, but it was also not designed to be a closing effect. As I left the stage to a wonderful round of applause, I felt I had the audience in the palm of my hand. I only hoped they would be ready for the rest of my show following the special presentation. Having this short break in the program, I took advantage of the moment to find a glass and jug of water and drape curtains, and saw the back of a large frame sitting on the easel. It had been uncovered and many of the people in the audience were now crying. On the edge of the stage were three small potted trees and just beyond that were a small group of people who had just arrived. The oldest lady was dressed in black and was emotional, distraught, trees. I approached closer, and I could hear the chamber president explaining how the loss of Terry Mayal, the founder of Bigfoot Campers, was a terrible loss not only to his family and friends, but also to the whole community of Vernon. I finally understand that seated in the front row was the widow who had not only lost her husband, but also a

OR THE HEAD CHOPPER

cousin and best friend in a tragic plane crash just days before! The special presentation was basically a wake in the middle of my show. Apparently, the small trees were to be planted in honor of those that had died so that future generations could remember these wonderful pillars of the community. I was frozen. I did not know what to do or say, but the worst was yet to come. As I stood there with a blank face, just behind the crowd, I heard the president ask for a minute of silence. Following this moment, which seemed like hours, he said, *"And now, back to the comedy and magic of Shawn Farquhar!"* It would be no exaggeration for me to say, *"I too **died** a little that day."*

I walked onto the stage, looked down at the sobbing mass of people who were grief-stricken and could not imagine that they wanted to see any more of my comedy magic show. I had saved the best effects for last, but could no longer even consider doing the CARD SWORD, JUMBO SIDEKICK with a handgun, or the HEAD CHOPPER. I sat down on the edge of the riser and spoke to the widow.

I expressed my condolences and explained I wasn't sure I should continue. She looked at me and said, *"It would be nice to laugh or at least smile a little."* So I stood up and gave it my best. Of course part of me wished I had just slept in. ♦

Agent 52, aka Fred, went a little overboard when his Commander ordered him to "blend in."

CLEVER DISGUISE

JASPER MASKELYNE

As Told by Ivan Amodei

In one of the darkest chapters in our world history came an unassuming hero Jasper Maskelyne. Did he help win World War II with his illusions?

In the 30s, Jasper became famous in the music hall scene with his feats of magic. He enlisted in the army, and never knew his skills and knowledge of legerdemain would actually become a integral part of magic's history.

At first, his abilities were overlooked, and he was sent to the Royal Engineers Camouflage Corps. Maskelyne believed if he could fool an audience merely yards away, he could easily fool an enemy who was a mile or more away.

The army sent him to North Africa where there was a shortage of soldiers and equipment. He worked tirelessly in Africa designing great deceptions to fool the enemy into thinking army tanks were just useless old broken-down trucks. He cleverly hid machine guns using mirrors. Mirrors also helped him create the illusion that a German warship was casually patrolling the river Thames. German planes were tricked into bombing the wrong targets.

In the North, thousands of tanks were made to look like harmless vehicles. In the South, he created two-thousand fake tanks, with sound effects and all to complete the illusion. A false railway line and water pipeline were constructed, mimicking all the characteristics to a tee.

MACHINE GUNS

All these feats paled in comparison to when in 1942, he threw all his efforts into convincing enemy Generals that the attack would come from the South, not from the North. Unexpectedly, when the real attack came from the North, it caught the Germans so off-guard, it forced them to retreat.

Whether this brief piece of Jasper's story is fiction or fact, Maskelyne's tale had enough buzz to captured the attention of Hollywood producers.

At one time, Tom Cruise was cast to play Jasper in a movie centered around his magic and skillful disguise techniques he used in battle. Because most of Jasper's work is loosely documented, some experts believe that his claims are exaggerated and made up. But if true, what an amazing story. ◆

A STICKY SITUATION

CHRISTOPHER HART

As Told by Christopher Hart

In the 80s, I had the opportunity to work at a place located on the Sunset Strip in Hollywood called *"The Body Shop."* Yes, it was a strip club, but actually modeled more after a famous classy French cabaret called, *"The Crazy Horse."*

The owner personally selected the acts, and a small group of talented magicians had already worked there before me. Names like Lance Burton, Joseph Gabriel, Norm Nielsen, and Goldfinger & Dove to name a few. It was an important opportunity for me, and I wanted to do well.

I shared a dressing from with the strippers. Yes, these are sacrifices you have to make at times in show business. It happened that I would go on at the same time every night after one of the girl's set. Since there was fire in my act, I wanted to soak lighter fluid on my torch and fire gimmick, as close to my performance as possible so it wouldn't evaporate before my act. I learned to time out my preparation perfectly to the last two songs of the dancer's set before me. Well, this one particular night as I was preparing my fire gimmick, it broke. My heart started to race as I tried to decide what to do. I had less than four minutes to solve the problem before her last song was over. There was no way to tell anyone about the problem, and I was going on regardless. I quickly pulled out

YES, IT WAS A STRIP CLUB

some Krazy Glue®, figuring it would take only a minute to set and fix the gimmick for at least one show. My hands were shaking as I squeezed the tube of glue onto the gimmick. Of course, in my

Next time I'm using scotch tape

I COULDN'T EVEN MOVE MY HANDS APART

hyped-up state, I squeezed too hard and out shot a huge glob of glue all over the gloves already on my two hands. The glue not only attached the fingers of the gloves together, but soaked through to my fingers as well. I now couldn't even move my hands apart, as they were super glued together. I could hear the music now halfway through the last song. There were only a couple minutes left before I would be introduced. The only choice I had was to pull as hard as I could to separate my glued glove fingers apart. Of course, as I now tried to pull the soaked gloves off my hands, they would reattach themselves again and again.

If it had not been such a desperate situation, it would have been funny. It took me tearing off a layer of skin as I ripped the gloves off my hands to get free. I tried to blow on the wet gloves to dry any remaining glue.

I quickly put the gloves back on, and ran to appear on-stage just in time for my introduction. My heart was still pounding through my entire act. Examining my fingers after the act revealed raw and red fingertips, taking a few days to heal.

Lesson learned. ♦

Its now or **dead** bird wiggle.

— THE OPENER *page 161*

Secret
AGENT

Nick Newin

As Told by Nick Newin

While seated at a bar, an attractive female patron came over and asked me if I was the magician that was to perform that night. I looked at my friend who I was having a drink with, and with a slight smile across my face said, *"Yes, I am."* Duty bound to answer in the positive. She proceeded to tell me all about a magician she had seen several months before. In particular, she expressed admiration for the miraculous manner in which he removed a shirt from the torso of a spectator. She asked me if I knew how this was accomplished and I replied, *"I did."* She beseeched me and said, *"Would you do it in the show tonight?"* I explained that this wasn't a trick that I regularly performed and wouldn't be doing it that night. Slightly crestfallen, she returned to her table in the club. My magician friend I was having the drink with said, *"Hey Nick, why not set it up and do it and just to surprise her?"* This sounded like fun, so we went into the green room and carefully arranged his clothes

JUST SURPRISE HER!

appropriately. My friend then went to the front of house to take his seat for the show. The show was going well. I went into the audience and approached my pal and commented on his formal attire

there was a serious sound of ripping!

He immediately appeared to become very vexed at this strange magician who was ripping at his shirt in public for no real reason. As he began to protest

registered what had happened, I began to laugh. The more he protested, the more I laughed. I just couldn't help myself. The audience must of thought I had lost my mind. I had approached

THIS TIME, THERE IS A SERIOUS SOUND OF RIPPING

and removed his tie in preparation for the stunt. That's when everything went very wrong. Having removed his tie, and unbuttoned several shirt buttons, I took hold of the shirt collar and gave it a very serious pull. It didn't seem to want to move. So I tugged again. This time

angrily, I looked into his eyes and realized exactly what had happened. I had been the victim of a practical joke — big time. The gag was on me. I realized, he had replaced his shirt in the customary manner and was now playing the innocent victim. The moment I

an apparent stranger, and destroyed the shirt on his back in a strangely hostile manner. Then all I could do was laugh about it! I later was introduced to his girlfriend the women that set me up. ♦

JUST
PATHETIC

PETER SAMELSON

AS TOLD BY PETER SAMELSON

We are now on land, and I am performing in a fabulous theater with a half-circle thrust stage, two steps down to the first row of the audience. You can feel a buzz in the room. The music starts and the curtains open. In all my elegance, I make my entrance. I do a spin so that my coat flairs, and somehow, inexplicably and impossibly, my foot catches on something. And the next thing I know, is that I am at the bottom of those two steps. I'm a bit stunned, looking up into the shocked face of a young girl.

The shattered image of the Great Magician lies in pieces all about me. And as I stare up at her, all I can think of is that poor girl has two more hours of show ahead of her. What must she be thinking? ♦

Did You Know?

By the 18th century magic as entertainment was well established in Europe.

One of the most famous illusionists was Baron Wolfgang von Kempelen. In 1770, he devised an automated chess player that took on all challengers.

Benjamin Franklin played against the machine in 1783 and lost.

THE BAT!

Stephen Bargatze & Roger Klause

As Told by Stephen Bargatze

It was one of my early years in attending the *invitation only* Obie Obrien's F.F.F.F. Convention in Batavia, New York. I noticed the front row of this close-up convention was made up of some very famous magicians. They were, however, all having trouble staying awake as the convention was coming to a close.

Occasionally, some performers needed someone to assist them in a trick and getting someone to volunteer was not always easy. In the front row, was the famous Roger Klause. He seem to be the go to guy for everyone.

He was a good sport. We saw Roger the whole three days taking card after card and trying to be a nice guy. I was chosen, for the first time, to close the F.F.F.F. Convention. No one was

WHO THE HELL IS STEPHEN BARGATZE?

as shocked as me to be chosen. My friend Eric Decamps who was with me, was sitting beside Roger as they introduced me. Roger leaned over and asked Eric, *"Who the hell is Stephen Bargatze?"* When I asked Roger to help me by shuffling the cards everyone was caught off guard when Roger said, *"No thanks, pick someone else!"* He seemed annoyed. Now of course, I couldn't let this go, and asked to crowd to give Roger a big hand for helping and one more time would not kill him. Really perturbed, Roger stood up and let the

crowd know that he had helped the whole convention of performers and just wanted to sit this one out. The crowd was now starting to divide up into sides. Some understood Roger's request in not participating, while others thought, as I did, *"Big deal, its just one last trick."*

Quickly, I told Roger *"Stop being an ass, and just give the cards a mix!"* The entire audience went dead silent. *"He just called Roger an ass,"* they thought. Roger clearly lost it and calmly walked up to me, took a small baseball bat that had been sitting on the stage and started

THE BAT

to beat the *Sh#@** out of me. In an effort to pull things back together, I decided to shuffle the cards myself. Just about the time Roger got back to his seat, I asked him, *"Then would you do me the honor of just…taking a card?"*

He did not think that was so funny and rushed the stage to furiously start the beating again. After a minute, he sat down. Just when you thought I could not take any more, I yelled out, *"Okay fine, well then, just think of a card."* He stormed the stage and went to town on me for the last time with the bat. I laid there almost lifeless, but also felt victorious that my sarcasm was able to stir up the *"Great Roger Klause."* The audience was simply in shock.

Well, this was all an elaborate prank we planned to play on all our magician friends. It really fooled everyone. My two friends, Obie O'Brien and Gene

Anderson, were quick to let me know how realistic the beating looked. After all, they knew Roger had method for hitting someone with a plastic bat, but never really inflicting any pain. Everyone knew it was a big joke after all. It was clear my good friend got carried away in his role. When I got home the next day, my wife counted over 35 bruises left by him.

As Roger would have said, *"One must suffer for his art."* My dear friend is missed by many. ◆

— *Read Full Story* , A FINAL BOW, *page 186*

QUICK BITS

Tommy Cooper

After a Royal Command Performance Tommy was introduced to the Queen.

"Do you think I was funny?" Tommy asked.

"Yes Tommy," replied the Queen.

"You really thought I was funny?", Tommy asked.

"Yes, of course I thought you were funny," said the Queen.

"Did your Mother think I was funny?" Tommy asked.

"Yes, Tommy", said the Queen, *"we both thought you were funny."*

"Do you mind if I ask you a personal question?" Tommy asked.

"No," replied the Queen, *"but I might not be able to give you a full answer."*

"Do you like football?" asked Tommy.

"Well, not really," said the Queen.

"In that case," said Tommy, *"do you mind if I have your Cup Final Tickets?"*

Finally, I am lowered to the tank, not completely yet, but stopped with just my hands touching the surface of the water.

This is when I am supposed to do my deep breathing, before going in to build up my lung capacity for the underwater part.

— TRAPPED UNDERWATER *page 143*

ARE YOU RICHIARDI?

— THE SWITCH *page 133*

no one was caught off guard when Roger said, *"No thanks, pick someone else!"*

— THE BAT *page 99*

She was visibly UpSet

— THE RING *page 139*

SHE LITERALLY FROZE

— THE ICE RINK *page 130*

Are you Hurt?

— GOING OUT WITH A BANG *page 103*

THE YEN

Gazzo

As Told by Gazzo

SO HOW DID HE KNOW?

Once I was doing a street show in Boston, MA. One spectator was a very wealthy looking Japanese man. His clothes, his watch, his briefcase, and everything about him reflected a man of extreme wealth. He was really enjoying my show and getting involved. After I passed my hat for contributions he came up to me.

He extended his hand for a handshake, and, in broken English said, *"I weawwy enjoyed yoo show. I have any American Cuwwency, I do not. Except foo dis."*

He opened his hand, and I thought that he was going to give me a huge tip, but instead all he had was a penny and a nickel. He said, *"It's for u hhat and kno it is not muuuch."* Then he gave me 10,000 Japanese Yen, but instructed me NOT to cash it until November 7th of that year. I had to wait seven months for a tip! I pinned the money to my notice board with a big NOTE next to it. **DO NOT cash** until the Nov 7th. Every now and again, I would pin something up on my board and notice the money, but never thought anything of it.

November 7th came at last, and I took the Yen and headed straight to the bank. I gave it to the teller and asked her to exchange it for USA dollars. She went to the computer and came back with $75 dollars. *"WOW! Great tip,"* I thought. I quickly asked her, *"So what would the 10,000 Yen have been worth back in April?"* She looked at her computer and said, *"Fifteen dollars."* I left the bank baffled and amazed at the same time.

How did this mysterious man know what the Yen's value would be seven months from when he gave it to me?

How did he know it would be worth so much more on Nov 7th? Until today, I still think about that. I had only one wish after leaving the bank: *that I had bought more Yen back in April.* ♦

GOING OUT WITH A BANG

MURRAY SAWCHUCK

AS TOLD BY MURRAY SAWCHUCK

I was 16, living in Vancouver, Canada, and starting my career in the entertainment and magic business. It was the *Children's Magician Competition*, and I really wanted to win this year's contest. I came up with this really impressive opening piece.

It was an illusion, where an explosion would go off, and I would suddenly appear standing in this diamond shaped opening.

I would be engulfed by smoke from the huge explosion which catapulted me onto the stage. After the major blast, I'd come stumbling down the stage, dressed in a full black & white tailed tuxedo, which was made to look like I was blown apart: shoes blasted open, shirt torn to shreds, and hair standing straight up to complete the grand comedic entrance. I looked a mess. Finally, when I hit the stage, I'd yell out, *"Kids, whatever you do, don't try this at home!"* That was the opening of my 10-minute children's magic act.

The show was *open to the public* and being held in the college's large theatre. That evening, the school was also full of students because night school was in session. The auditorium was packed. I was the first act of 12 to go on-stage and compete.

The music started, the curtains opened, and the huge explosion hit. **Boom!** Smoke filled the stage and theater. I appeared on-stage as planned inside the illusion. I stood up to roaring applause. I jumped down off the illusion, said my opening line, and thought, *"Wow, this went perfectly!"* One second later, EVERY fire alarm in the college went off! We had to immediately evacuate the entire building! People were scrambling to run outside. You could hear all the fire trucks arriving. I couldn't believe the chaos I just created. I began walking up the steep hill, where I was instructed

ARE YOU HURT?

to go, and was completely shocked at what I saw: **2800 people**, (*students and teachers*) all standing on the sidewalk. I evacuated the whole college on the

Fred wished he had renewed his insurance policy.

evening of the school's final exam. Firemen rushed over to me because of my dishevelled appearance asking, *"Are you okay, are you hurt?"* Making the incident seem all the more tragic, real and funny at the same time.

I assured them I was fine. And it was all part of an act. Apparently, the illusion worked to fool the firemen who believed I really **blew myself up**.

When I told them the truth, that I was doing a magic trick, they laughed hard about it. You know who was not laughing? The judges. They were not impressed and were very upset I forgot to tell them I was working with explosive materials. At least then, they could have turned the fire alarm lasers off before the show.

Needless to say, I didn't win ANY awards for my performance that night. But I got a story for a lifetime. ♦

You're Killing Me

ALDO COLOMBINI

As Told by Aldo Colombini

As magicians, we sometimes have the opportunity to work for unusual audiences. One day, I was booked for a private party at the World Famous Magic Castle in Hollywood, California. When I got there, I realized the audience were people belonging to the *"Suicide Supporters Survivors Group."*

Basically, everyone in the audience either attempted suicide or was stopped while trying to. Now I thought, *"What do I have in my act that may be inappropriate?"* Let's take a look. Well, I have a thick rope that is tied into a noose. I could take it out and say, *"I'm going to need a volunteer!"* I could do the RAZOR BLADE trick for them and say, *"Does anyone want to test to see if these are indeed real razor blades?"*

How about asking for a volunteer and then bringing out the GUILLOTINE illusion? Even though all these options

You killed us!

were really tempting, I finally came to the conclusion that it was probably, not, a good idea. I removed a couple more gags that weren't suitable (*pretty much everything*) and did my show. The audience had a great time. After the show, I packed and went to the parking lot to get my car. The spokesperson of this group ran up to me and said, *"Aldo,*

you were so funny. You KILLED US!" I said, *"Well, wasn't that what you were trying to do anyway?"* ON THE INSIDE!!!

OUT LOUD, what I really said was, *"Thank you! I'm so glad everyone enjoyed the show."* Yes, I was nice, but the temptation was great. Here's the lesson learned: select your material carefully and remember, as my dear friend Roberto Benigni said, *"Life is Beautiful."* ◆

Fred would later regret going to the Hypnotist's show.

THE HYPNOTIST

DAN MCKINNON

AS TOLD BY DAN MCKINNON

I was on a cruise ship touring the Caribbean with my family. One day, I shared a drink with the ship's hypnotist at the bar. We became friendly and decided to pull a prank on a guy sitting next to me.

Since the ship's magician was not too far away and everyone around us could see him, I decided to take advantage of a casual question. I asked a person sitting next to me, as I pointed to the magician, *"Have you seen the magician's act?"* He said, *"Yes, I really enjoyed it."*

I then told this *unsuspecting victim*, that it was my dream to learn a little magic and the magician taught me how to make a golf ball disappear the night before. I asked if I could show him the trick. He agreed to watch. Little did he know what I was going to do with him.

I proceeded to make a golf ball disappear, although, badly. Trying to make it seem as though I was just learning. I said, *"See it's gone, it's now back in the hand it started in."* He replied, *"That looked pretty good."* I think he was just being nice. I then told him, *"I have a surprise for you. I've been working on doing the same trick, except in someone else's hand."* I put the ball in my victim's hand and told him to turn it face down. I said, *"Shake the hand that contains the ball, as you do, it will go up your sleeve, around your back and into your other hand."*

I continued, *"Now, I'll do the hard part, and make it go back!"* I shook his hand and showed him the ball was back in the original hand it started in. We all laughed, as he understood it was a big joke. What he didn't know was all this distraction was so that I could steal his

SEE, ITS GONE!

watch off his wrist. I succeeded in the theft, and handed the watch to my *new* hypnotist friend behind me. I walked away. The hypnotist got up and started talking to the passengers. By now, he

was wearing my victim's watch on his wrist. He asked a group of people (*including my victim*), *"Did you see my show tonight?"* Our victim said, *"Yes, but my wife could not be hypnotized."*

The hypnotist explained, *"Well, it doesn't always work with large crowds and sometimes Flash Hypnosis works much better one-on-one."* The man replied, *"What is Flash Hypnosis?"* He replied, *"I'll demonstrate. Face me and put your left hand against mine, as if to give me a high five. Close your eyes."* He snapped his fingers twice within a few seconds.

The hypnotist then asked him, *"How much time passed between snaps?"* The man replied, *"Just a few seconds."* The hypnotist said, *"No, 40-seconds passed."* The guy laughed and said, *"No way!"* The hypnotist answered, *"Then how did I have the time to remove your **wristwatch** and place it on my wrist?"*

The man literally **freaked** out! He said, *"It was the greatest thing he had ever seen."* Simply powerful. I did ALL the work and HE got ALL the credit.

I can guarantee you this — that ***man*** will never forget what happened to him the day he was hypnotized for just a few moments for as long as he lives. ♦

Did You Know?

CHUNG LING SOO

In the 19th century, many magicians presented themselves as Chinese magicians, including the American Magician, William Robinson, *aka* Chung Ling Soo.

Chung once unveiled a wonderful Chinese banner for his audience, unaware that it was an advertisement for a funeral parlour. Embarrassing to say the least. *A fact that is both bizarre and chilling once you understand the circumstances of his death.*

Read his story, READY, AIM FIRE, *page 233*

By now he was bathed in sweat and panting in exasperation, but Houdini still could not. . .

— LOCK PICKING *page 86*

REAL MAGIC

DOUG HENNING

AS TOLD BY IVAN AMODEI

In the early 1970s, Doug Henning rose to stardom at lightning speed, only to disappear at the height of his career. Why did he leave magic so suddenly and a life of fame he had worked so hard to attain?

To unlock the key to this deep man, and see further into the choices he made, you have to look back at a rich life of education and committed spiritual longing.

Doug became enthralled with magic at the young age of six. By 14, he was already performing on local television programs and doing private parties.

Doug also wanted to become a doctor. And after attending McMaster University, he enrolled in medical school. He was captivated with psychology courses and studied the power of perception. But he decided to wait two years before attending medical school and try his hand at his passion for magic. Nevertheless, he used his new found knowledge from his studies to create, build and detail-out *new* illusions that had never been seen in the world of entertainment.

He had entered into a magic career *full-time* now, and hard work was to follow. His goal of become a doctor had been left behind.

His dedication paid off when he performed in *"Spellbound"*, a musical that combined an intense story line and magic. It broke every box office ticket sale in Toronto, Canada for its time.

During his run with the musical, Doug captured the attention of some New York producers who made him an offer that he could not refuse — to take his show to Broadway. A huge opportunity.

He re-worked *Spellbound* and it was an incredible success. *The Magic Show* ran for four and a half years earning Henning a Tony Award nomination.

The following year, Doug was approached by NBC to perform on

SEVEN EMMY NOMINATIONS

50 MILLION VIEWERS

television and it would be shot in front of a live audience — Doug's forte.

One illusion he performed on television which catapulted him into stardom was his re-creation of Harry Houdini's dangerous WATER TORTURE ESCAPE. It instantly made Doug a household name. He was now a huge star. In December 1975, Doug Henning's television special *World of Magic* captured the attention of more than 50 million viewers and won him the *Christopher Award* for Outstanding Achievement and earned him a contract with NBC who agreed to air the television shows every year.

For seven years, his TV show delighted millions of viewers which resulted in Doug also being nominated for seven Emmys. In 1976, Doug moved to Los Angeles, and started his own production company. He worked hard on creating and building his own illusions. In a 1984, he returned to Broadway with his solo show, *Doug Henning and His World of Magic*. All the hard work paid off again, as Henning won the prestigious *Georgie Award* from the American Guild of Variety Artists for *Entertainer of the Year* and, *Magician of the Year* from the Academy of Magical Arts & Sciences.

Suddenly, in the mid-80s, Doug vanished from the magic scene completely. He wanted to discover if there was another side to magic. Was there *"Real Magic?"* He went off to follow and study with his spiritual leader Maharishi Mahesh Yogi. He NEVER returned to the stage. Many of his illusions were sold to prominent magicians including Siegfried & Roy.

REAL MAGIC

While studying with his master, one of his most important fascinations was examining transcendental methods for **actually** *"levitating"* without resorting to *any* magic mechanisms.

His passion to find these answers through spiritual and metaphysical techniques was the motivating force behind his leaving the magic world cold. Could he discover if there was indeed *"Real Magic?"*

His search was cut short, as he passed away at the young age of 52. If there was ever a person who could find the answer, it was Doug. Did he find what he was looking for?

I believe he did. ♦

Did You Know?

JACOB MEYER

In 1774, Jacob published the first magic book by an ***American-born*** magician *Little Treatise on Strange and Suitable Feats*. Most of the British Colonies of North America were under the strong influence of Puritanism, which frowned on all idle amusements as works of the devil. Magicians were outlawed in some colonies. Only in Dutch New Amsterdam were such entertainers well received and permitted to perform.

The general lack of acceptance in the colonies may have prompted the first outstanding American magician, Jacob Meyer, to make his reputation in Europe during the second half of the 18th century.

He adopted the name of his birthplace, Philadelphia, and traveled Europe entertaining royalty and the general public under the name Jacob Philadelphia. He even reached Russia, where he performed his illusions for Catherine the Great.

A HOT ACT

CHRISTOPHER HART

AS TOLD BY CHRISTOPHER HART

Triple Espresso. It was a three-man comedy show, and I played the magician character *"Buzz Maxwell."* The act consisted of numerous funny magic bits and gags all strung together.

One night during the waving of the torch trick, some sparks flew off and landed into my magic bag sitting next to me. Slowly my bag began to emit small wisps of smoke as I continued with the act. As the volume of smoke began to increase, the other actor in the show tried to get my attention by pointing at my bag. He was waving and jumping up and down. I remember thinking he must have had too much coffee. When I didn't notice my accidental combustion, he came up and under his breath said, *"Your bag is on fire!"* I looked over slowly, and saw my bag emitting smoke. I ran over and proceeded to try and blow out the fire.

This blowing had no affect as the flames began to increase higher and higher out of my case and out of control The audience erupted into laughter, thinking it was all part of my act. The more I blew into the bag, the higher the flames rose, the louder the laughs got. Upon seeing my dilemma, the second actor, with panicked look in his eyes, came up to help me. I handed him the bag now filled with fire and whispered to him, *"Just take it off stage!"* My thought was that he would handle it backstage and put it out. When I got backstage the magic bag was now fully engulfed in flames and my actor friend was desperately trying to make a fire extinguisher work to no avail. We found out later it was actually empty.

YOUR BAG IS ON FIRE!

Suddenly, I realized that inside the bag was a full container of lighter fluid! So I quickly reached in and pulled out the flaming newspaper from the torn and restored trick I had performed earlier. I then dove down for the bottle of lighter fluid protecting it from the exposed flames, and luckily averting a full out explosion. I stomped repeatedly at the burning embers left in the bag and finally was able to extinguish the remaining flames.

The actor and I ran back on-stage and continued to finish the first half of the show. We hoped the audience would think it was just a comedy bit, as the character was a bit of a bungling magician. Later in the second half of the show, my character in the need to raise money has a line that said, *"And I collected fire insurance."*

Needless to say, it got a huge, sustained laugh and helped cement in their mind that it was all part of the show. After all, I was hot that night for reasons I would not like to repeat. ♦

GET A
ROOM

THE MAGIC CASTLE

AS TOLD BY JAMES BENTLEY.

I have been in the magic industry for a long time and, I think I have seen it all. Being a professional magician, you really do meet the craziest people and see the funniest things. I think this story is amazing because it involves Ivan Amodei, your book author, The World Famous Magic Castle in Hollywood, and some of those crazy people that I just mentioned.

I also work as a Host at The Magic Castle and my job entails not just introducing acts in the various rooms, but also policing and making sure that the guests are safe and nothing dangerous or illegal is happening on my watch. Its like I'm the *Secret Service* of The Magic Castle with these little ear pieces in. I am wired up so that at any time someone can talk to me without me having to pick up a phone.

On one memorable night, I was in the middle of an introduction for Ivan's show. I began to introduce Ivan in the Close-Up Room, and at the exact moment, I was to say his name, I heard someone yell into my earpiece, *"Jim. get upstairs NOW to the Palace of Mystery, there are two highly intoxicated people doing THE DEED!!!!! in line."*

My face was frozen with this image, and I sat there unable to speak. I fumbled out some nonsense, perplexed what I should do next. Needless to say, I screwed up Ivan's intro irrevocably and he had no idea what was going on.

The audience had no clue why I was so distracted, you see no one knew another host was yelling in my ear. After a few moments of utter blundering, Ivan came out with a look of bewilderment and said, *"NICE Intro JIM!"* as I raced out of the room, I yelled back, *"Gotta go!"* I ran upstairs to find they were, in fact, doing THE DEED!!!!! As politely as I could, I interrupted them and said, *"Could you both please refrain from your enjoyable after hours activities for when you arrive home."*

It was definitely a combination of perfect timing and outrageous circumstances that happened one night at The World Famous Hollywood Magic Castle that I will never forget. ◆

> ## WHAT, WHERE?

BUNNY
SCARF

WOODY PITTMAN

AS TOLD BY WOODY PITTMAN

Over the years I guess I have lots of stories I could tell, from a person dropping dead in my audience to a little girl peeing on-stage. However, I think the most memorable thing that ever happened to me happened very early on in my career.

I was just out High School and had been doing magic shows since I was 14 in various venues around my home town of Ellettsville, Indiana. One day I was asked to give a performance at the local junior high.

At the time, I was getting a bit of a reputation as a good magician. I think it was mostly because I was the only magician in the area. At this stage in my magic career, I was doing some illusions in my show from a SHADOWBOX to a SUB TRUNK. I had just started using livestock in my show too. I had a couple of doves named Gertrude and Heathcliff and a bunny named Bunny.

During this particular show, I had just finished my great performance of the SUB TRUNK which was like watching The Pendragons in slow motion.

Now it was time for my big closer. As the music started, I grabbed what appeared to be a large butterfly net. I was about to perform DOVES FROM NOWHERE. I spotted an imaginary dove in the air made a swoop with the large net and a dove magically appeared inside the net and then landed on a tray held by my assistant (*my older sister*). I made another swoop and another dove appeared and landed next to the other

EVERYONE LAUGHED HYSTERICALLY

dove on the tray. I picked up the doves and then approached a small cabinet on a pedestal known as the INDIAN DOVE CHEST.

The INDIAN DOVE CHEST is a small little ornate chest painted in bright colors with Indian themes on all sides. It's made to hold a rabbit in the main chamber and a couple of doves in the bottom of the box.

When the lid of the box is removed all four sides of the box collapse exposing a rabbit sitting on the bottom of the box where the doves are concealed in the secret compartment. The chest is designed to fit a bunny on the smallish

size. However my bunny, did not fit these particular requirements. When I got *Bunny,* I was told he was a dwarf rabbit which meant he would only grow

to put the birds in the chest, the sides collapsed, which caused the lid to hit *Bunny* on the head. This scared *Bunny*, and *Bunny* leaped from the chest onto

the fact, that *Bunny* had claws like a cat. And when he climbed up my chest, he sank his claws into my chest every little step of the way, to get around my neck. My white shirt took on a bit of a pinkish glow.

BUNNY HAS A GLANDULAR PROBLEM

up to be very small, perhaps not much bigger than a large guinea pig. *Bunny* must have had a glandular problem as he really never stopped growing, and on that particular day, I had to kind of wedge him in the chest in order to perform my great illusion.

Whilst I approached my beautiful INDIAN DOVE CHEST, in which, I was going to place Gerdy and Heath, the cabinet started to shake as if we were having an earthquake. And just when I was close enough to be able

my chest. He preceded to climb up my chest and wrapped himself around my neck like a scarf. There I was, standing in the center of the stage with a bird in each hand and a rabbit wrapped tightly around my neck.

So I stook, paused, and said, *"Good Night"* and walked off stage while ***everyone laughed hysterically***. Obviously, I was quite embarrassed by this out come, but could really only laugh just like everyone else. What really hurt (*other than my pride*) was

A few days after that memorable performance, I thought it was best to not do magic of any kind with livestock again. So I set Gertrude and Heathcliff free and gave *Bunny* to my sister who turned him loose on her farm where he lived a comfortable life in the barn.

At the time, the path of being a comedy magician was not for me. However, I must admit, if I could have had this happen in every performance today, without the injuries, I think I would close every show with this wonderful, funny routine. ♦

chapter
five

Pigs, strange coincidences, a bit of luck, bridezillas, freak situations and rings

MISHAPS TO GLORY

GENE ANDERSON

AS TOLD BY GENE ANDERSON

It was my fourth year in a row to be one of the speakers at the Michigan Project Management Institute's Professional Development Day. My speech was on humor (*Life Is Too Important To Be Taken Seriously*).

I usually do a magic trick at the end, and this time it was Kevin James' BOWL-A-RAMA, the effect where a sketched bowling ball becomes real and falls out of the drawing pad onto the floor. Very startling and funny.

I wasn't the opening speaker, and in the rush to get my materials in position prior to my start, I somehow missed getting my music on my laptop cued to the right track. When the wrong music came up for my finale, I said, *"Hold on, let me get the music cued up correctly."* I went down beside the platform stairs where my music system and computer were on the floor. A potted palm was partially blocking decent access to them. I barely squeezed past the plant, and the microphone transmitter on my belt accidentally hooked the tree and knocked it over onto me. Audience started laughing. Number one accident. More to come.

I got the plant all standing back up, got the music cued, and then went back up on-stage where the everything went beautifully. Finally, the Bowling Ball production got a huge reaction when it hit the stage with a loud thump. Suddenly, the ball began rolling forward and toppled over the front of the stage. Once again, big laughs from everyone. But this time, the ball fell directly on my laptop computer on the floor. Not so funny anymore, at least not to me, but people continued laughing, as they thought it was part of the act. The *PowerPoint* presentation on the screen went completely black. Funny again, to them, not me. Well, my computer guy said, *"Its toast, totaled like a car in a crash. No more laptop."*

But there's no question about this:.Because of a comedy of errors, ***I was the highlight of their development day!*** From now on, I will charge more the next time I do the Bowling Ball trick and also remember to clear the area of expensive electronic equipment. As Garrison Keilor said, *"Who needs dignity when you can be in the entertainment business?"* ◆

FUNNY?

Direct HIT

Dick Barry

As Told by Dick Barry

One afternoon, I was performing at a men's service club luncheon. A great effect I did was borrow a dollar bill from a spectator, tear it up, give one piece back to the person (*receipt*) and place the rest of the torn bill loosely into a dove pan (*a metal pan with a lid*). The pan was lit on fire and immediately covered with the cap. Now for the magic.

I quickly removed the lid, and a beautiful white dove was now there — the torn bill had vanished. The dove has a small, yellow envelope tied around its neck. This envelope is handed to the spectator who loaned the money. After tearing open the envelope, the spectator finds their original dollar bill restored, except for the missing corner. The *receipt* corner fits the bill perfectly. An unbelievable piece of magic that always gets great reactions. On this particular afternoon, when I removed the lid from the pan, the dove got spooked (*maybe from the lights*) and took off into the large room filled with over 100 men, all seated and scattered about at 12 large round tables. Well, the dove circled the room over and over, and over, and I was beginning to wonder if it would ever land? Well, it did land. And what was unreal was it landed *directly* on TOP of the spectator's head who loaned me the original bill "WOW!" I thought. A miracle just happened, but I was not saying a word. It was all just a part of my show. I walked off the stage, approached the man with the dove on his head, and handed him the envelope from its neck. He found his restored dollar bill and his piece fit perfectly. To say, the audience was stunned, shocked and blown-

WOULD IT EVER LAND?

away was an understatement. The two most popular comments I received were, *"That was the best trick we have ever seen, ever — hands down!"*

The other was, *"How did you train that dove to land EXACTLY on top of HIS head?"* My consistent reply, *"Its the miracle of magic, isn't it!"* ◆

THE SECRETARY

GOLDFINGER & DOVE

As Told by Goldfinger & Dove

We once took a vacation and forgot to tell our agent where we were going. Then our agent got a call for a very important engagement that we had been expecting.

temporary secretary who was there just for the day said, *"I know where they are!"* He went into her office and asked, *"Really, where are they?"* She said, *"They're in Hawaii. Would you like*

answered the phone. Curious as can be, he headed back into his temporary secretary's office and asked, *"How did you know they were in Hawaii?"*

She looked up and casually said,

WHERE ARE THEY?

He immediately called us at home and was surprised that he could not get in touch with us. He called every phone number he knew including all of our connections and could not find us. Frustrated, he yelled out into the air *"Where in the world are Goldfinger and Dove?"* From an outer office, a

their number there?"* He was amazed and confused. How did this temporary secretary, who was in just in for the day, know where we were more so than he did? He went back into his office and called the number she gave him. After hanging up the phone with us he was perplexed. He couldn't believe we

"Oh, I'm their next door neighbor!" Dumbfounded by this weird coincidence, the agent went back to his desk shaking his head. I guess some things are just meant to be. The show was a great success. ♦

Now the bastards will never know how its done

— QUICK BITS *page 131*

So I went ahead with the bit.

— THE JOKER *page 39*

The whole audience burst into laughter while I stood there, dumbfounded

— WHERE ARE YOU? *page 51*

It was the Ritz Hotel in Aspen. *"Do you do birthday parties?"* **Oh I love those calls.** *"How old is the birthday child?" "16 and his brother is 10 and his sister is 6."* **Yuuk. I was about to beg off with my** *"I don't do kids parties"* **rap when the concierge broke in and said,** *"It's royalty."*

— A NIGHT TO FORGET *page 124*

that was the **worst** F**ing thing I ever saw! Should have done a top cover pass. Geez, why the hell did you do it that way, **THAT WAS TERRIBLE!**

— I HATE CARD TRICKS *page 215*

A Night to FORGET

Doc Eason

As Told by Doc Eason

It was the Ritz Hotel in Aspen. The call came in. *"Do you do birthday parties?"* Oh I love those calls. I asked, *"How old is the birthday child?"* They replied, *"He's 18, his brother is 16, and his sister is 6."* Yuuuk! I was about to beg off with my, *"I don't do kids parties"* rap when the concierge broke in and said, *"It's royalty."*

Visions of Princess Diana and the boys danced in my head along with some dollar signs. I asked, *"Well, when is it?"* They replied, *"Tonight."* Royalty, I guess, expect people to be waiting for their call.

So I shot them a number that reflected the fact that I was going to have to rearrange my busy (*day off*) schedule. The concierge would have to get back to me, but that it didn't seem to be an unreasonable amount. As I hung up the phone, I wished I had quoted more. In retrospect, I should have turned it down completely. Within a few minutes they called me back. I was on. He said, *"Be there at 6pm for a security check."* I would go on shortly after that. They wanted 30-40 minutes. Piece of cake

DO YOU DO BIRTHDAY PARTIES?

I thought. I wired up my pop up tie, shuffled a couple of decks of cards, and put together my doctor's bag for a house call. I arrived promptly and was directed to one of the smaller ballrooms. There was a buzz in the air as I met the video guy who was to shoot this memorable event and several members of the wait staff assigned to the room for the evening. Just past six, a swarthy man in an expensive suit enters the room and stands by the door. I'm no expert, but I would have to say that he was packing heat. A moment later, a man appeared

Too cool for school

in a open neck, crisp white shirt and a toothpick in his mouth.

Blond, crew cut, he is American. He is clearly a career soldier type who has moved onto a much more profitable line of work. Head of security for some Saudi Prince. He was concerned about what was in my magic bag. Explosives or pistols? He didn't seem to be too thrilled with the switch blade that I use for the lemon trick. So I found a regular steak knife and warned them when, in the act, the knife would be used. I didn't want him to think I was going to attack the kids. I got the feeling that

if I didn't handle the knife correctly, I would be shot on the spot. He grilled the others too, and we all apparently passed inspection. He then told us that the family just had lunch. It was 6:30pm and that it might be a while until they came down, but that he would give us some warning. A couple of hours past.

We all stared at each other in disbelief. We couldn't leave because they might show up at any moment. Muttering to myself, I set the chairs and made my little performing area and spent the next four hours entertaining the staff and the video guy. Finally at about 10:30pm,

the swarthy suit slinks into the room again. He instructed us to be ready in 15 minutes. We all stood up a little straighter and make sure our ties were on right. A half an hour later, I was more than a little perturbed. They still hadn't shown. I hoped to be home in bed with a fat paycheck by now!

Two more guys with suits and heat came in and stood on either side of the door. Ten more minutes, the entourage blast into the room. Talk about an entrance! Little brother and sister came in and made a bee line to my table. Dragging chairs right up and sat right smack in front of me. The other chairs were dragged to about 10 feet away and at an angle away from me. Completely destroying the setup it took me five hours to set up! My feeble protests were drowned out by a flurry of language I had never heard before amongst

THE PREPPY TYPE

most of the people in the room. The immediate family was closest to me. They were high ranking Saudis, but I didn't recognize any of them. The little girl simply stared at me blankly. Her slightly older brother was a little more attentive, but a bit precocious. The birthday boy was a preppy type with a *"too cool for school"* attitude. He was being fawned over by a young woman who was dressed in a mini skirt and had a pair of white leather boots that went above her knees. There was no one else in the room that could have been remotely close to being his mom, but this woman looked more like a hooker!

It could have gone either way. In the seats they had dragged to the far wall, six older folks politely sat down with their hands in their laps. The men were dressed in business suits and the women are wearing American style dresses. They were far enough away from me that I couldn't really engage them in any of the activities. As far as I knew, they didn't speak English either. As the show unfolded, it became painfully obvious that most of people right in front of me didn't speak or understand English. My funniest lines were met with blank stares. Also I discovered that they didn't even have playing cards in Saudi Arabia. Since most of my act are card tricks, I felt myself nose diving into the tank. Time slowly crawled. This show seemed to be taking hours to get through. I looked at my watch it had only been 10 minutes. The cut and restored rope with the little girl is met with only mild amusement. She couldn't understand anything I said.

Big Time! All I wanted to do was get out of there. I wasn't even that concerned with collecting my fee. I started my finale, the lemon trick. I didn't even care if I got shot when I pulled out the

with anyone in the room. The birthday boy sidles up to me. With what had just happened, I didn't know if he is going to stab me or ask me what a deck of cards was. He leaned in and said into my ear,

I WAS SWEATING PROFUSELY

Nothing was working. I was wearing my popup tie and since that seemed to be the only thing that *"got a rise"* out of the crowd, I was popping it a lot. I was also sweating profusely and my head was spinning. The show was tanking.

knife. I almost hoped for a gunshot so I can end the agony. Somehow I made it through. The party moved to the cake phase and I was madly throwing stuff into my bag hoping that I could get out of there without having to lock eyes

"How do you make the tie go up?" A 30-minute ordeal and all he wanted to know is how the tie works! The whole scene was surreal. The room was spinning. I was seriously considering a career change while being pestered by

I agree

a **16 year old Saudi Prince** about my popup tie. I was close to just bolting out of the room screaming, when one of the folks from the back of the room approached me and in English said, *"I enjoyed the show. You know I'm Joe Steven's sister."* Whaaat!?!? These six folks are somehow all from Wichita, Kansas and know Joe from the famous Steven's Magic Emporium. Joe is Lebanese and apparently *"connected."* I had entered the *Twilight Zone*. The only saving grace about his ordeal was, I thought, all these people would simply return to the Middle East and no one here would be the wiser. But no, not only have Americans witnessed this, but they happen to be related to one of America's foremost magic dealers!

I took little comfort in the check I received. I should have stayed home! ♦

Quick Bits

Back in the early 80s, Lori my wife and I had a 13 minute dove act at Legend City Amusement Park, during our second show one Saturday afternoon, I pulled the third dove out of my tux only to find he died.

He was fine as I loaded him, but died moments later. So when I pulled him out I knew right away something was wrong. I stuck my thumbs under his wings flicked them up a few times then handed him to Lori and under my breath told her not to perch him for the finale as he was not going to stay perched!

— Mike Finney

GUINEA PIG

HARRY KELLAR

As Told by Ivan Amodei

Harry Kellar was an American magician who worked theaters and stages all over the world during the late 1800s and early 1900s. Kellar came to fame before Houdini and in a way, paved a way for Houdini to become a household name.

One of his most famous effects was his NESTED BOXES. Kellar would borrow six finger rings from various audience members. He would load them into the barrel of a pistol which he would aim and fire at a chest hanging from the ceiling of the stage.

Inside this chest is another smaller chest and so on, six chests deep. The smallest one is opened and five rings are found each tied to ribbons with flowers. But where is the sixth ring? One January 17th, 1904, *The President of the United States*, Theodore Roosevelt took his children, daughter Ethel and his three sons, Archie, Kermit and Quentin to the Lafayette Theater to see Kellar perform. Kellar performed his signature piece and borrowed six finger rings. Ethel was the owner of the sixth ring. When Kellar finished the first sequence, he revealed five finger rings tied to a ribbon and rosebuds inside the smallest nested box.

But Kellar did not return Ethel's ring, but returned the others. Immediately, Ethel shouted in a voice that was heard over half the theater, *"Papa, I didn't get my ring back. Tell the man I want my ring!"* Kellar then brought a bottle down into the audience and asked everyone to have a drink. He magically poured

PRESIDENT ROOSEVELT LAUGHED

water, wine and whiskey all from this bottle. With a hammer, he cracked the bottle open and out popped a little white guinea pig. Tied to the guinea pig's neck, on a blue ribbon was Ethel's ring. He asked Ethel, *"Would you like to keep the animal as a pet?"*

Smilingly, she agreed. Kellar wrapped the guinea pig in paper and handed it to Ethel. When she opened it, the guinea pig had changed into bouquet of pink roses.

The President and Mrs. Roosevelt laughed, but the boys were not happy. *"Shucks, we wanted the guinea pig,"* said Kermit. ♦

THE ICE RINK

GEORGE SCHINDLER

AS TOLD BY GEORGE SCHINDLER

And then there was the show in the Ice Palace. The stage was set of sheets of drywall atop the ice at one end of the skating rink. It was October and while it was cold outside it was still warmer than in the arena.

IT WAS REALLY COLD IN THE TRUNK

We went outside from time to time to warm up. As he was preparing to set his table on-stage, one of the acts spilled the water for his IN THE NEWS on top of his prepared ANDERSON PAPER TEAR. So he had one trick left. We skipped his act, and pulled out a hair dryer and started work on drying all the papers. In the meantime, Al DeLage was almost finished with his act, but we needed a few more minutes. Margaret walked on to the stage and handed him a few more props and he calmly added more to the act. The papers were not yet dry so Jeff McBride stepped into his spot early. It was really cold in the rink.

A few minutes before it was needed we were trying to get his duck into a freezing DUCK PAN. I had no doubt she didn't want to go.

Jeff gave me an unhappy glance when the prop arrived on-stage a bit late. The newspapers seemed ready to go and the act was on next, but the closing act had his daughter ready in a DOLL HOUSE. She decided to get in early to get used to being in the box. And she literally froze. The act opened and her two parents pulled a crippled and crying girl out of a beautifully colored prop. ♦

THE SAW

RICHIARDI

AS TOLD BY IVAN AMODEI

Richiardi Jr. (*often billed just as Richiardi*), was the stage name of magician Aldo Izquierdo. He became infamous for his dramatic and gory stage presentations of classic stage illusions. Renown for his closing piece: SAWING THE WOMAN IN HALF illusion. He started a very large, oversized buzz saw and lowered it through a woman assistant already laying on a table on-stage. As it pierced her body, blood and guts splattered everywhere, including all over his medical white coat.

A very gory scene, as well as, really realistic. Each and every audience he performed this for consistently screamed in terror. After, Richiardi even allowed spectators to line up and inspect the massacre. In one performance, at Madison Square Garden, it took nearly an hour for everyone to complete their inspection of the bloody and gruesome site.

By the way, the assistant was always his daughter. ♦

An American magician was on board a Greek cruise ship about 30 years ago, on a long contract. He carried a couple of illusions and they gave him an empty adjacent cabin in which to store them.

One night, he heard some noises coming from that cabin. He got his key, and opened the door to find the Captain and his Chief Engineer checking out his ZIGZAG illusion. They laughingly said, *"We just wanted to know how it worked,"* and left in a hurry.

The magician was so teed off, he and his assistant pushed the ZIGZAG to the back of the ship and threw it overboard, as he muttered,

"Now the bastards will never know how it's done."

— Ron Wilson

QUICK BITS

What happened to him on April 15, 1984 goes down as a tremendous tragedy in entertainment history.

— A FINAL BOW *page 186*

THE SWITCH

GEORGE SCHINDLER & RICHIARDI

AS TOLD BY GEORGE SCHINDLER

It was a large shopping mall and while we were setting up our illusion show, I looked for the contact person who had our check. The lighting was good, the sound was working nicely, and I found the man I was looking for. We had an hour before show time and the man came up and asked, *"Which one of you is Mr. Richiardi?"*

It suddenly dawned on me that the agency that sold the show (*since they couldn't get the real thing*) sent my *"World of Illusion Show"* instead. Now what do I do. I told him, *"I not Richiardi."* Needless to say, the man was pissed. I pulled out my contract and showed him who I was and that this is where were sent to play. I said, *"Sorry sir, we'll pack up and leave."* But people were collecting outside the theater area

and he replied, *"Okay, let's do it, I'll straighten it out later."* So I said, *"But we need to be paid first."* He pulled out his checkbook and gave me the fee. He had already paid a big deposit to the agency. It was a really good show. We finished the show and went home.

A week or so later, after depositing the check we got a little surprise letter from the bank. You guessed it! He **Stopped Payment** on the check. I should have

WHICH ONE OF YOU IS RICHIARDI?

known better. It took several months with litigation through AGVA for me to recoup enough to cover the payment to my acts. And the agent's reason for *"Stopping Payment"* on the check. He said, *"I could have booked the same acts cheaper."* So much for being young and anxious. ♦

ELVIS?

SHAWN McMASTER

AS TOLD BY SHAWN McMASTER

To begin this story, I think I should share with you my high-level of dislike for Elvis impersonators. A few years ago, I was performing at a huge Mardi Gras-themed event. The people who booked me really went all out. No expense was spared, and it showed.

A variety of entertainers, including the singing group The Tokens (*of The Lion Sleeps Tonight fame*) performed at this function.

I was scheduled to go on after The Tokens, but I was informed during their performance, that an Elvis impersonator who was scheduled for later in the show had another engagement that he had to get to, and I was being bumped to allow him to go on before me. I was told that he would be on for about 10-15 minutes. He did 45. Now maybe it's just me, but I have never understood the reason for Elvis impersonators. Before I start, let me go on record here by stating that I am a fan of Elvis and his

work, and maybe shortly after his death, Elvis impersonators may have had their place. If for no other reason than to be thought of as giving homage to *"the greatest entertainer to ever touch the*

AND BEING AN ELVIS IMPERSONATOR

IT WAS A NIGHTMARE

hips, and talk in between numbers in a voice that sounds only marginally like Elvis at best? And being an Elvis impersonator does not allow for creativity or original invention. They have to sing like Elvis. If they don't, then they aren't impersonating Elvis.

It was a nightmare, and he started to lose the crowd. This man went on and on and on. So much so, that I had to fight the urge to shove barbiturates down his throat and sit him on the toilet in the men's room just so that I could finally go on.

Okay, that's a cynical exaggeration (*hold onto your hate mail*), but the crowd despised him, as did the other performers. ♦

Story continues with *"Organized Chaos"* on page 136.

stage" (*a tag-line, in itself, that smacks of Houdini-like boastfulness*). But after almost 33 years since the man's death, it seems to me that it can no longer be considered *"homage"*, but instead, just plain *"sad."* There is no longer any purpose for these entertainers. It's not like they are offering anything original. They're singing Elvis' songs. They have to. And Elvis Presley only recorded and performed so many songs.

Do we have to constantly subject ourselves to listening to someone who's not Elvis sing Hound Dog, swivel his

ORGANIZED CHAOS

MARC BACHRACH

AS TOLD BY MARC BACHRACH

Now I will add, as Paul Harvey used to say, *"the REST of the story."* Elvis? on page 134 continues here. The *"huge Mardi Gras-themed event"* Shawn just described was, of course, a wedding reception.

The bride had a well documented stage fright measured at truly phobic levels of intensity.

So much so that the actual wedding had been held in another city with only six people in attendance a month before.

I had been hired as a stage hypnotist to include her in my performance and hypnotize her to unleash the world-class quality singing voice no one had heard for over ten years because of this psychological condition. At that time her new husband, a Nashville country music star, would join her for a duet that would bring the house down and leave tears in everyone's eyes. Shawn's stand-up comedy/magic performance was slated to be my warm-up act, and would end with the bride being *"flown"* around the room, carried in Shawn's arms after he *"stripped"* down from his suit to the blue leotard hidden underneath the hysterical climax to a very funny routine. Imagine, then, the bride's *"delight"* when *"Elvis"* brought her into the center of the room ALONE, put a microphone in her hand, and LEFT her there for five minutes to fend for herself.

Why, you ask? Because a few moments before he had realized in his megalomaniacal stupor that his next costume change was still outside in his car and he needed to retrieve it RIGHT THEN! It was all the poor woman could do not to faint dead away as she trembled and suffered through waves of acute panic and embarrassment. Luckily, her husband, a rather glib and

---

THIS WAS A RUNAWAY TRAIN!

THE BRIDE WAS VOMITING!

charismatic fellow, carried on while no music played and the crowd became as unfocused as Elvis.

True to the *"runaway train"* nature of this wedding, still another character in the massive cast of entertainers, a large, overweight, oddly dressed female minister decided that she, too, would need to perform out of order and go on before our Magic and Hypnotism segment. Of course, mom agreed to her demand, too. As this bizarre chanteuse warbled through some less-than professional sounding original material accompanied by her out-of-tune guitar, ANOTHER half-hour of **how much can this audience possibly**

tolerate passed by interminably, with Magician Shawn, the band, and I off in the corner agreeing that this WAS the worst planned and executed wedding reception any of us had ever been part of. As each excruciating moment ticked of with no end in sight, we entertained ourselves with whispered wisecracks, and shared fantasies of demanding *"combat pay"* afterwards.

Yes, you guessed right: *"Mom"* thought she could do ALL this herself: pull off a complex, entertainment-heavy 300 person reception without a wedding planner or coordinator. Four hours before, I knew pretty much where we were headed when I walked past

the Mardi Gras Juggler I had hired to greet the guests. And there was *"Mom"* — on the verge of a nervous breakdown racing around the room ALONE with no help, putting decorations on tables and dealing with vendor crisis after vendor crisis, clearly having the least fun of anyone I've ever seen at a wedding reception. Not the enthusiastic, vivacious, thoughtful woman I had met two months before. An exhausted, embattled, and besieged amateur who had completely lost control of the event long before the people walked through the door. In retrospect, it was like watching a preview of FEMA managing the aftermath of Hurricane Katrina. Well, to finish our story, *"Elvis"* left the building with the two bimbos he had set out to impress and bed later. The minister assaulted any sensitivities, patience, and politeness the crowd had

HOW MUCH CAN THIS AUDIENCE TOLERATE?

left in reserve. Five minutes before the magician was to take what was left of the *"stage"*, the bride and groom had completely disappeared!

Forget about the perfect set-up we had painstakingly orchestrated, there was no way to delay OUR part of the show until they were found! So, no bride and groom during the entire warm-up act! The bride finally was found in the bathroom finishing her vomiting, and returned shaken to the main room. Needless to say, I did not even consider involving her in the show at this point (*the volunteers were already on-stage*

and hypnotized, and she was far too fragile). The crowd, which had been extraordinarily responsive, gracious, and involved five hours before, was completely fried by this point, and I performed the fastest, briefest version of my show humanly possible. What troopers. If it had been me out in that audience, I might have been throwing things by then and screaming for the band to return. Obviously, the entire purpose for our entertainment (*hypnotizing the bride out of her acute stage fright to recapture the joy of singing*) was completely obliterated.

The only saving grace was that *"Mom"* had enough sense (*and overwhelming feeling of defeat*) to realize that this outcome was completely her doing, and did not renege on the payment of our normal princely sums.

As she numbly handed over our payment envelopes, I resisted the twisted urge to remind her of how many times I had gently encouraged her to consider getting a coordinator to help her.

Just smiled, thanked her for the opportunity to be of service, and congratulated her on producing on a beautiful reception for her daughter and new son-in-law. ◆

THE RING

STEVE COHEN

As Told by Steve Cohen

I STILL HAD **25** MINUTES TO GO.

In 2007, I was invited to be the featured performer at a high-society fund-raiser in Manhattan. Two-hundred very wealthy people were gathered in the ballroom of a private Park Avenue clubhouse, and I performed a modified version of my Chamber Magic show.

Having presented this show over 2000 times by that point, I felt confident throughout the performance. Until the rings routine. For years, I've featured the HIMBER LINKING FINGER RINGS (*where I link together borrowed finger rings*) in my shows. This time, though, one of the borrowed rings snapped in half. Fortunately, it was during the *"unlinking"* stage of the routine. I had already linked three wedding rings, and displayed them to the audience. As I was disengaging them, I felt something crack like a pretzel. I looked into my cupped hand and saw that one of the rings — which contained dozens of antique rubies — had broken in two. Several of the tiny rubies had slipped free. Thinking fast, I returned the first solid wedding ring to its owner, followed by the second solid ring. Now the tricky part. I had to return the third broken ring, but didn't want to ruin the rest of the performance. After all, I still had another 25 minutes to go. And 200 people watching.

So I hid half of the ring in my right fist, and gripped the other half at my right fingertips. Keeping the ring half-concealed, I advanced forward to show it to the last spectator. Recognizing the visible rubies along the edge, she confirmed to the rest of the audience that it was indeed her ring.

As soon as she verified that the ring was hers, I dramatically placed it (*with the other broken piece*) into my jacket pocket. This got a big laugh — the audience thought I was joking. They thought, I had intentions to steal the ring. I simply said, *"Don't worry miss, you'll get your ring right back before you leave tonight."* I left it at that, since it was a somewhat satisfactory

comedic conclusion for the audience, and continued on with the next 25 minutes of the show. Nobody knew that anything went wrong.

After the show was over, the ring's owner approached the platform. I took her off into an adjoining room, and asked her if she had enjoyed the show. She said, *"Yes, it was wonderful."*

I replied, *"I'm glad that you enjoyed the show because there's a slight problem. I broke your ring."* She answered, *"That was my mother's wedding ring."* I froze for a moment.

I showed her the two pieces of the ring, and she was visibly upset. Fortunately, though, she was not the type of person who made a public display of her disappointment. I promised her that I would have the ring repaired. Thank goodness, I have a strong working relationship with one of Manhattan's top jewelers. Over the next two weeks, he melted down her gold ring, and rebuilt it with the original rubies (*which had all been cleaned and remounted*). There were several missing rubies that had fallen during my show, but my jeweler located matching rubies that filled in for the ones that got lost in the floor cracks. The ring was now Tiffany-quality. It was better, much better than the original. And, it was made using the same gold and stones that were originally contained in her ring. Needless to say, she was thrilled.

I learned a lesson — don't borrow any more family heirlooms! ♦

QUICK BITS

I watched a very green magician was making his big stage debut on one of those horrible school auditorium stages.

You know the ones, they're about five miles high, with steps on either side. Nobody wants to come all the way up and help the magician. Finally, this magician had enough. When he asked a gentleman to come up on-stage, and the guy said, *"No."* He begged, cajoled, and then tried to shame the guy into coming up.

He asked for a round of applause for the guy, but he still refused to budge. Finally, the magician asked him what his problem was? The answer, *"You see, I'm in this wheelchair?"* He wanted to die!

— Curtis Kam

chapter
six

Life or death, card cheating, planes, trains and automobiles, sexual harassment, stuffiness

While watching the news, Fred's mom wished she had NOT told him to "Follow his Dreams" and forced him to finish medical school.

WATER TRAPPED UNDER

STEVE DACRI

AS TOLD BY STEVE DACRI

I know what your thinking just what is a close-up magician doing in a story about Houdini's death defying underwater escape? Trust me. I often wonder this myself.

This whopper of an idea turned into a mid-act *"faux paux"* or *"error"* call it what you will, I like to refer to it as the *"unplanned moment"* which nearly killed me.

It was all over the news, CNN, ABC, and my mother's VCR.

I remember my publicist at the time who suggested it, *"We need you to do a huge publicity stunt for a client, you know, hang from the roof in a straight jacket or jump out of a plane, the normal sort of death defying activities that certify one's insanity and gets great press. Any ideas?"* For some reason, I believe fear of heights being the motivating force, I blurted out *"How about re-creating Houdini's most famous underwater trick?"* Her eyes lit up like that doll in those *Chucky* movies. *"That would be perfect, can you do that?"*

I'm sure you know I said, *"Sure."* I never really thought anything would come of it, but a few days later, with a contract and cash in place, I was soon off to discover the secret to this great escape I agreed to do. Surely there were all sorts of safety mechanisms in place, secret air tanks. Something. I set out to visit Walter Gibson, confidant and prolific magic author for so many famous magicians. He was also my friend, and he had shown me original notebooks that belonged to Houdini. I flew to New York, and armed with a bottle of the finest Scotch there might have been two. John Gaughan taught me all I needed to know to do this crazy escape. He shared the knowledge of Houdini's

---

IT WAS ALL OVER THE NEWS, CNN, ABC AND MY MOTHER'S VCR

actual methods and the reality that I could actually die in this contraption. The date was set. March 25th, Houdini's birthday. And the location was to be

HOUDINI'S BIRTHDAY

Hollywood Boulevard, a block from The Magic Castle and next to Houdini's star. Johnny built the tank, and he was my advisor for this trick at Radio City. I spent eight weeks preparing for the event, doing what I was about to do right now. I would climb a ladder, stand at the edge of the top of the water torture cell and jump into the ice cold water, paddle around then go to the bottom, and hold my breath for as long as possible while Johnny and his staff stood by timing me (*and laughing uncontrollably*).

The ritual went something like this: I would drive out to Glendale, California, about an hour's drive. I would light up a Cohiba, turn up the Stones and hit the California freeway system. By the time the cigar was finished, I was parked by the front entrance to Johnny Gaughan's place. I started out at around 30 seconds. After six weeks, I was easily holding my breath for two minutes.

By the time I actually did the trick for the first time, in front of hundreds of onlookers and dozens of press cameras and live on ABC television, I was ready to go longer if necessary. The escape happened without a hitch, and I will never forget the feeling of relief and

accomplishment when I staggered out from behind the curtain. Dai Vernon was one of the first to congratulate me, and he said, *"Houdini would be proud."* Some things you never forget. That was a year ago. Now I am in training again, about to do it for the second time, this time at Radio City Music Hall in New York City, in exactly three days.

Today, as I stripped off my clothes in the Johnny Gaughan factory, I was enjoying the feeling, more than ready to do it again on that historic stage I had always dreamed of walking on. This would be my final practice before the tank gets shipped to New York. I decided I would not actually do the trick again until we got to New York, and give it a run through in the afternoon rehearsal on the actual stage. Instead, I was merely chaining my hands to a large cement block and jumping into the

I was holding my breath for two minutes

tank. The game was to escape from the chains before I ran out of air. I aced it in less than ninety seconds.

We flew to New York the next day, and rehearsal began at noon. I went to the theatre in the morning to check the props and I spent a lot of time sitting on the edge of the largest stage I had ever seen, looking out at the magnificent theatre and the 6000 empty seats, and frankly, wishing this water torture thing was over already.

Rehearsal never fully occurred on the stage with the water torture cell. I spent two days rehearsing the illusions with two female assistants dancers, Rockette types. They had never been in a magic show before, blocking out the moves for the illusion sequence. I was doing thin model sawing, crystal casket, levitation, ZIGZAG and sub trunk, typical stuff for a close-up magician.

When it came time to rehearse the tank, the elevator that makes the tank appear was broken, so the teamsters uttered those famous words, *"Don't worry, we know what to do."* My rehearsal took place without the tank. The teamsters tied my feet to a thick rope and lifted me about 500 feet above the stage. A chalk outline indicated where the tank would be. They practiced hoisting me up, then over the tank and down into the tank. I overheard them taking bets that I would not come out of the tank alive.

I will always remember the excitement of the first glimpse of the crowd, every seat was filled and the energy was indescribable. I vaguely recall the butterflies in my stomach when I heard my name announced, and that incredibly long walk from the wings to center stage. I opened with a few jokes.

The first one, nobody laughed. Flop sweat was in full production. Before I started to venture into the second joke, the laughter from the first joke began. The place was so huge that the sound

HOUDINI WOULD BE PROUD!

of the applause took a while to reach the stage. It was bizarre. I adjusted, the laughs continued, and I could feel the magic working. The illusion sequence was marvelous, I guess. I would have much preferred to be doing paper balls over the head. When the sequence ended, with an audience member on-stage for the sub trunk, I did just that. The laughter shook the floor of the stage. The on-stage orchestra was screaming. What a great night! Now it was time, I ran offstage to change out of my tuxedo and into a rented tuxedo because only a complete fool would jump into a tank of ice water in their finest evening wear. While I am changing, Walter Matthau's son David comes forward and acts as the host, explaining the seriousness of the trick as the tank slowly rises into view. I return to the stage and New York City Police Captain O'Malley locks my hands into his own handcuffs, then he supervises as Johnny Gaughan and his team lock my feet into the top of the tank. Johnny leaned over and asked how I was feeling. I smiled and said, *"I'll feel a lot better when this one's over."* Or something like that, how am I supposed to remember this? Next thing I know, the teamsters are hoisting me upward, and I feel like a circus performer on the way to the high wire. I look out at the upside down scene in front of me. I am swaying back and forth, in a tuxedo, shackled and handcuffed, as the band plays and everybody waits.

I recall taking a *"mental photograph"* of this special moment as I hung there, upside down. Finally, I am lowered to the tank, not completely yet, but stopped with just my hands touching the surface

DON'T WORRY, WE KNOW WHAT TO DO.

of the water. This is when I am supposed to do my deep breathing before going in, to build up my lung capacity for the

waited until I realized they were not lowering me, so I let my breath out. All at that same moment, they suddenly

Then it went dark, and I knew the curtain had been pulled around the tank, my signal to get busy. The first thing

> ## I'LL FEEL A LOT BETTER WHEN THIS ONE'S OVER.

underwater part. I could see that the tank had been overfilled, and thought, *"I hope that's not going to be problem later."* I took my final deep breath and signaled to Johnny, who yelled to the lead teamster, *"Do it."* I'm holding my breath and waiting, relaxed as I could be according to Houdini's notes, if you become nervous or excited, you lose at least thirty seconds of air. I waited and

lowered me down into the tank. I didn't panic, I was calm, but I thought how unfortunate this would soon turn out, with no possible chance for me to avoid the outcome. Without sufficient air in my lungs, I will surely pass out. I began to see the faces of all the friends I knew were in the audience. I recall thinking about how disappointed they were all going to be.

I did was the emergency move I was taught, to bend myself in half and stick my head up to the top edge of the tank to catch a breath from the air trapped under the top. There was no air, of course, only water. I bent back down, relaxed and set about releasing myself. At the two minute mark, the curtain will drop, they will look at me, lifeless, I assumed, and then the all-so-embarrassing emergency

I HOPE THAT IS NOT GOING TO BE A PROBLEM LATER.

rescue would begin. Somehow, using strength I didn't know I had, I kicked my feet so hard that I was able to pull free from one side. The cold water had numbed my ankle, so I felt no pain at the time. I inverted myself and escaped. I can't tell you how, only that when I was finally out, I was now standing on the stage, between the tank and the curtain. I'm supposed to lift the curtain and walk forward triumphantly. I lifted the curtain, walked forward and I discovered that I was facing the startled orchestra. I was so disoriented that I didn't realize I was at the rear of the tank, not the front. I quickly turned and ducked back under the curtain, made my way around to the front of the tank, and made my valiant appearance. I could barely walk, so I hobbled out to the center of the stage as the crowd

QUICK BITS

This magician's show was really bad. It was terrifying to watch. After the show, the woman who hired him got up on-stage, took the mike and apologized to the entire audience for his horrible show.

She repeated his name, making it clear that no one should *ever* consider hiring him in the future, and told everyone how he had led her to believe that he was the best in the business. She apologized again to everyone for them having to sit through that show..

Following a reaction like this, most guys would have written off the fee and left. But, this guy demanded she still pay him, and threatened to sue the woman if she didn't. Unbelievable.

— Curtis Kam

went wild. It was a heady, exhilarating and totally foolish thing to do. I soaked in the emotion, the feeling, and the sights of that moment. I think I smiled for days. And I limped for about a month. Looking back at that potentially disastrous evening, I don't think I will ever forget the moment when I realized I was probably going to pass out in front of 6,000 onlookers. But the memories of that night are great ones, and I have since performed this illusion two more times, for corporate clients that paid me an obscene amount of money to recreate it. That was all before Jan was a part of my every day life. The President of the Magic Circle Michael Bailey of Magic Circle Headquarters in London asked me, *"Would you ever consider doing this on Stephenson Way in front of our building?"* Before I could open my mouth, my beautiful wife said, *"Not on your life."*

Part of me wonders, secretly, if I could still get in the tank and do the escape again. Holding my breath for over 2 minutes would be the biggest challenge, the escape part is simple for me.

But could I actually pull it off again? I guess, for the right price, and a lot of top shelf Vodka martini. I certainly could be persuaded to find out. ♦

A TEXAS SHOWDOWN

MAX MAVEN

AS TOLD BY MAX MAVEN

I was headlining a comedy nightclub in Houston, Texas. I'd worked there a number of times before, and it had always gone well. It was opening night, and for whatever reason, attendance was a bit sparse. Not a problem. You just have to work a little harder to keep the audience cohesive.

However, on this particular evening, such was not to be the case. The club had a thrust stage, which meant there were people on three sides. Most of the customers took seats facing the front of the stage. Off in the Stage Left corner of the room was a pair of people. It was clear that they'd chosen deliberately to sit apart from the rest of the audience. The male of the duo was dressed in cowhand attire. While the opening acts were performing, I observed that he was drinking beer. A lot of beer. It seemed

HE'S GOT AN EARRIN!

prudent to keep an eye on this one.

Sure enough, ten or fifteen minutes into my set, the cowpoke noticed my pierced ear — a far more controversial fashion accessory back then. And he suddenly bellowed, *"He's got an earrin'!"*

This wasn't the first time I'd received such a comment, but it was the most hostile delivery I'd yet experienced. Ever prepared, I even had a line to deflect the statement. I'd smile and

TIME STOOD STILL FOR A MOMENT!

say, *"When you can afford diamonds this size, I figure you can wear them anywhere you want."*

That usually took care of the issue. But on this night, I was wearing other than diamonds, so the line wasn't viable.

I decided that the best policy was to simply ignore the guy. After all, he'd overtly separated himself from the others, and the rest of the crowd was enjoying the show. And then, a few minutes later, he shouted again, more angrily, *"He's got an earrin'!"*

Now it was getting uncomfortable. Handling a heckler is a delicate task. Handling a heckler in the form of a drunk and pissed-off cowboy is almost like surgery. I ignored this second outburst and carried on, but it was certain that if he shouted again, I would have to acknowledge him. As I continued talking to the audience, in my head I was rapidly weighing my options, because I'd only get one chance to direct the course of events.

Worst-case scenario: He might leap onto the stage and assault me, before club security could stop him.

And, as expected, he blared again, *"I said, he's got an earrin'!"*

Time stood still for a moment. All eyes were now on the ranch hand, and I was on the verge of making my initial response, when something lovely happened. Sitting at ringside, front and center, was a burly guy with a full and grizzly beard, wearing a plaid flannel shirt and a truck driver's cap. Glaring at my heckler, he slowly stood up. He was big. Really big. Figure well over six feet, and probably at least 300 brawny pounds. And he said, in a no-nonsense tone, *"Hey. I've got an earrin'!"*

The heckler having been silenced for the rest of the night, the big guy sat back down, and nodded his head toward me as a friendly invitation to continue my show. Which I did.

And the best part of the story is that from where I stood, I could plainly see that the big guy did not, in fact, have an 'earrin'. ♦

I'm sorry I did not answer your email sooner, but I was in the hospital.

— A KNOCK OUT *page 167*

MIXED SIGNALS

R. Paul Wilson

As Told by R. Paul Wilson

We were doing things that movies were made of. The movie *Oceans 13* looked like a biography of our real life. A pack of guys playing and working a casino to find its weakness. We had a small crew. I was spending eight hours a day practicing with a binary keypad hidden under my trousers.

This little computer counted cards to keep track of what cards were dealt and what were remaining. Our first live game was a disaster. Our signaling system, at that the time was based on a series of gestures. Some of these are particular to each crew, while others were more universal. For example, running your fingers through your hair, from front to back is the signal for everyone to hit the exit and immediately leave the casino. This happened on that first night. We were all busy *keying-in,* when I noticed my crew getting up to leave. I was the only player left with a computer strapped to my back! Pushing my chips into my pockets, I left the table and

WHAT HAPPENED?

headed outside too. No one was there, so I hailed a taxi and went to our hotel suite. Someone had obviously gotten *spooked*, but I had completely missed their signal to leave. I was also totally unaware of any problems with the staff or management. From where I was

sitting, it had all been going well. **What had I missed?**

When I arrived at the hotel, the first thing I asked was, *"What happened?"* Everyone was staring at me. My crew mate asked, *"What do you mean, what happened?"* I was baffled. *"I'm sorry, but I missed the signal,"* I said. Everyone's mouth dropped open. *"Missed it? It was you who gave us the signal,"* he snarled back at me.

As it turned out, I had a habit of running my fingers through my hair, from front to back when I was nervous or under pressure. I accidentally evacuated the entire gambling crew.

After that, we changed the signal to make sure I didn't send everyone home early again. ♦

MAKE IT
HAPPEN

Kostya Kimlat

As Told by Kostya Kimlat

You've heard of the golden rules of magic? First, practice. Second, don't repeat a trick. And third, don't tell the audience what you're going to do ahead of time.

That's probably one of the better parts of my job — that I never have to own up to my mistakes that I never have to tell anyone, *"I'm sorry, I screwed up."*

However, I am about to tell you of a recent escapade where I wasn't so lucky. Where I did have to tell my audience what would happen ahead of time and where everything did, in fact, go wrong.

It's a story of a close-up magician who went overseas to do an illusion show, and came back home a whole new man. The client for this particular show had hired me the year before for their annual week-long conference/getaway,

and I had given them everything I had: days of dazzling close-up and hours of stand-up magic. It was a wonderful week in the French Caribbean, and I was honored to be invited back to join the CEO and the franchise owners, this time in the Canary Islands off of

FRENCH CARIBBEAN

Spain. Wishing to impress, I pitched another week-long production of magic. I asked my friend and fellow Orlando magician, Darren Rockwell, to join me, and we hired Victoria Leigh, who had worked with us on some previous shows, to be our lovely assistant.

We planned two large stage-shows for that week. The first would be an opening ceremony, where we would warm up the crowd, do an interactive prediction and finish with a production of the CEO. The second show would be a more formal *after dinner* banquet,

which would feature two illusions. The client was a company out of Sweden that manufactures the finest beds in the world. Not just any beds. Truly the best handmade beds in the world, which takes a lot of effort. The initial idea was to use a *"bed illusion"* that Darren had

PLAN B

been performing for a few years. It was a perfect concept: we would present the *"new"* bed to the audience, produce a beautiful girl levitate her (*as you drift away to sleep in this new bed you'll start to feel weightless*) and make her vanish (*like a dream*). This, along with another illusion, THE CRUSHER, were to be the two big highlights.

We had specific limits on size and weight of baggage we could bring with us. We contacted a shipping company that promised us that all 600 pounds of magic would arrive safely as long as we shipped them three to four weeks ahead of time. Our weeks were filled with nonstop work. After solid rehearsals with all of the large props, we packed up the cases and shipped the two illusions, all by themselves, to the Canary Islands, where we would meet up with them.

Countless *pre-show* emergencies had taught me that I want to arrive at a show with everything planned out, so that I can relax, focus, and be in the moment. I had been on a long, stress-free show streak and was looking forward to another wonderful week in paradise doing what I love.

While still at home, Darren designed a wonderful collapsing ASRAH that would eventually be the key to our success. With a few trips to the local hardware *"magic"* shop, we put together a simple, yet effective three-panel screen for the CEO production.

The frames for the screen could be taken apart and put together on the spot. Everything could be packaged up in one tall box, and with a bit of payment for oversized luggage, could be checked in for the flight over to Spain.

The real troubles began a week before we left, when the shipping company called to notify us that while they could deliver the illusions to Madrid, they had no method of transporting them to the small Canary Islands.

There was a *"Plan B,"* but it was going to severely cut into our budget. We decided to fly into Madrid a day early, pick up the illusions and go to the airline that was going to take us to the islands, and pay another $1,000 plus in overweight and oversize baggage fees. We imagined every possible scenario, deciding finally to deal with it all when we arrived in Madrid. We never had to deal with any of that because the illusions never arrived in Madrid at all.

When we landed in Madrid as

planned, we still had hopes of the illusions arriving on time, but were doubtful. What about our checked luggage for the opening show?

A tall, skinny cardboard box emerged from the trap door and precariously tumbled down the carousel. The metal frames we had measured and cut were sticking out of one ripped end, but at least they had arrived! We had our three-screen production so we knew we could pull off the opening show and have a great start. Upon arriving on the Canary Islands, our first show was on a Sunday morning and we kicked things off with a bang. The side-stage was ready for us when we arrived, the CEO was excited to hide where necessary, and a few quick rehearsals with him and the screens made us feel confident in his production. Remembering the magic from the previous year and seeing that the production had grown in size, all of the attendees were eager to be astonished.

The first show went off without a hitch. The opener jump-started the crowd, the interactive piece got them on the edge of their seats, and undoubtedly when the CEO appeared they were standing on their tiptoes cheering and applauding.

they had wished would show up for the convention still hadn't been allowed to get through customs.

When the phone rang early the next day, we picked it up, holding our fingers crossed. It was nothing but the sound of our dying excitement. We weren't getting our illusions, and we didn't have a single hope of presenting the grand production we had originally

WE WEREN'T GETTING OUR ILLUSIONS

As Sunday night drew to a close, we had our last hopes dashed that the illusions would arrive in Madrid airport on Monday morning. Speaking to our client, we found that they were experiencing similar problems with shipping and importing. Items that

pitched to the client. We now had to do an hour-long show without the 600 pounds of props that we had hoped would be delivered. We had our work cut out for us. We had already written and rehearsed the effects. The girl was to appear, levitate and vanish. Standard

---

CAN YOU KEEP A SECRET?

stuff. But now that the *modus operandi* had vanished, we started to brainstorm other possibilities. The appearance of the girl could be re-worked, but the vanish — and the beautiful, steel bed, a secret wedge base that was crafted to conceal and deceive — there was nothing that could substitute it.

We ambled around the hotel. There were beds all around us, flown in for the conference not just to add to the décor, but to show the franchise owners the fine details and handicraft that goes into each bed. Perhaps we could use one of their beds for the illusion.

We stood there at one of the bed displays, admiring the handiwork of two Swedish builders whom we had befriended when we first arrived. Now they were constructing a whole giant bed, layer by layer, making it come together, as if by a magic of their own. Darren and I looked at each other with a glimmer of hope and asked the two of them, *"Can you keep a secret?"*

We explained our dilemma and asked them if they could possibly build another bed, a *"custom one"* in 24 hours? While they worked that night, we also rehearsed and planned until 4am. When we woke up two hours later and rushed back to the theatre hall, we were speechless.

The bed was a masterpiece. Solid pine from Sweden, hand-cut and measured to our specifications. The guys had stayed up until 5am to complete it and it was an absolute work of art. Measured, cut, angled, nailed, supported and constructed like the finest pieces in a Vegas showroom. We now had just a few hours left to practice before show time. The client had requested the show be performed after their day-long meetings and before dinner at 6pm. The clock was ticking. I think it was raw energy and an unwavering awe of the age-old dictum, *"the show must go on"* that

gave us the drive to succeed. We spent the morning preparing the supporting pieces for the show, and we created performance of strolling close-up magic. Much to my amusement, several people came up and said, *"The trick* first has to learn how to play nice with others.

That month taught me many great

DO THAT TRICK WITH THE TWO RUBBER BANDS AGAIN!

45 minutes of great stand-up material. The remaining 15 minutes were for the grand illusion at the end. That day flew by, and at six o'clock in the evening, we went on-stage. The room was packed. Performing the bed illusion was an absolute delight. Here I was, originally a *card-trick-geek* at heart, presenting a levitation of a girl as a half serious pitch to a room full of people who halfway wanted to believe that what I was telling them was true. They loved it! We spent the next day recouping, cleaning, and packing up before the next evening's

with the girl was amazing, but can you do that trick with the two rubber bands again? I wasn't able to sleep for two days thinking about that!"

After that performance, I made a few brash statements: **I'm never doing illusions! I'll never ship anything again.** I've done both since then and not because I had to, but because we are artists, and I've been told that there are no mistakes for us — only lessons. The close-up magician who wishes to expand his parameters, dipping his toes into the theatrical waters of stage magic,

life lessons, including the appreciation for the work that illusionists have to do, the necessary skill and ability to rely on other people, and about the wondrous things you can produce when you work with others.

If you want to grow as a performer, open yourself up, make yourself vulnerable. Just make sure you've got a back up plan. ♦

THE QUESTION YOU HAVE TO ASK YOURSELF IS:

Do I want to go to jail for that?

— HIGH STAKES *page 170*

The OPENER

RICH MAROTTA

As Told by Rich Marotta

I was new to the magic business. I had a ten minute act. Nothing special, but I did end with a good bird production. Once, I got a gig as the novelty act on a fund-raiser show.

The kind of a show where they sell more tickets than they think people will come to. Since the show is for charity, they assume many businesses will buy tickets and hand them out. If a lot of people do come, they put on an extra show. This show was at the Masonic Auditorium in San Francisco. A massive venue that held a few thousand people.

I got there early, as my contract specified to do a *run-through* to check lights and sound. When the stage manager saw I was a magician, he told me that they had a magician there the night before and that his bird flew away. They tried to find it, but couldn't, and the magician was forced to leave without the dove. It was no surprise to me. The Air Conditioner was not working and the theater was very hot. I knew the dove flew away to cool off. I got myself ready for my set. I also finished some last second preparations directly behind the curtain just a few moments before being introduced. It included loading my dove into its holder and into my suit.

"This next act is a magician," the emcee announced. He then proceeded to tell a bunch of magician jokes. One after another. A few minutes went by, and the dove gave me a *"its hot in here"* wiggle, so I took him out of my pocket to cool off, but I kept the dove in the holder and held him in my hand.

When the emcee finished with all his magician jokes and mentioned, I was from New York City, I again, reloaded

---

"ITS HOT IN HERE" WIGGLE

the dove into my jacket. After another few minutes of New York City jokes, I had to remove the dove a second time. Finally, the emcee got around to my credits. *"It won't be long now,"* I thought, before I got on-stage, so I loaded the dove again. But the emcee went on, and on, and on. He had me working at venues I never heard of. I couldn't unload the dove for a THIRD time because I didn't know when he would finally stop his bottomless banter and the curtain would finally rise.

I waited. And waited. And waited. I felt sweat running down my neck. *"It's hot in here,"* I remember thinking. The dove also gave me a *"it's now or dead bird"* wiggle. The curtain finally lifted. It was just too much for the dove's safety, and I couldn't wait any longer. I had to produce him now and not at the

end of my act. So, I opened my show with my **CLOSER!** Once the dove was free, it took off. Probably to cool off, like the other dove. I saw it flying into the rafters toward the bright spot light.

Beneath the light, I could see a small white dot. I automatically knew it was the other magician's dove.

Now, my dove saw the other dove, got freaked out, and immediately turned around and flew back towards me. The other dove saw my dove and flew towards it. Both doves were flying directly at me. I held up my *right-hand*, and my dove landed on my right finger. I held up my *left-hand*, and the other dove landed on my left finger.

The audience went **WILD!** They were screaming and yelling! I got an instant standing ovation. They're thinking, *"Okay, this guy is unbelievable! He*

comes out, immediately produces a bird, it flies off, splits into two, then they come back and land on his fingers. WOW!" They couldn't imagine what the rest of my act would be like. I had a lot to live up to. Unfortunately, when you **open** with your **CLOSER** and its the BEST closer you've ever had in your life, the act can only go one direction from there — *Down Hill* — which it did.

The rest of my act was the most painful nine and a half minutes of my life. I ended to **mild** applause.

After the show, the guy who booked the acts came up to me and said, *"Hey kid, that trick with the one bird that turns into two. Keep it in the act!"*

The other dove belonged to Bobby Clark, a great old-time magician. I managed to return his dove to him and thanked him profusely. ◆

DOWN HILL

IT'S AN
ILLUSION

Curtis Kam

As Told by Curtis Kam

I was a consultant for an illusion show in Waikiki, Hawaii. We were worried about how one of the illusions looked from the front row. I decided to go into the audience and watch from there. I sat next to a group of people excited to see the big show. They asked me if I could do a quick trick for them. I did one simple card trick. The illusion show started and it was a multi-million dollar extravaganza, with all the lights, fog and dancing girls you could ever want. Lots and lots of illusions. 90 minutes of pure magic. After the show was over, I asked a guy at the table, *"So how did you like the show?"* He looked at me and said, *"How did you do that card trick? That was amazing."* So much for big expensive, flashy illusions. ♦

I was booked to do strolling Magic for a Major corporation. I wanted to impress the CEO and his guests. In the middle of the routine, I turned to one of his family members who was a gentleman with his arms at the elbows out of view under the table. I said, *"Sir would you please shuffle the cards."*

He looked at me confused, and said, *"Well, that will be a little difficult"* and raised his arms up and from the elbow down both arms were amputated. I have never apologized so profusely in all me life.

— Rob Rasner

HE SAID TO THE LADY WHO SIGNED HER CARD, *"Your card is gone!"* **THEN HE SAID,** *"It will appear in any room in this Castle that you would like it to appear. For instance, the Library, the Kitchen, the Woman's Room and so forth."* **She thinks and replied,** *"The Woman's Room!"* **He immediately answered,** **"GO!"**

— A CRAPPY TRICK *page 203*

SIMPLY SHOCKED

TOM BURGOON

AS TOLD BY TOM BURGOON

Back in 2002, I was hired to do a stand-up show for Anheuser Busch. I did the performance and everything went beautifully.

After, I headed back into the country club for a quick beer. The place was packed, and as soon as I got to the bar, one of the Busch guys yelled to the bartender, *"Hey Larry, show Tom that card trick you do!"* Larry pulled out a deck from the behind the bar, and proceeded to lay out three rows of seven. I let him do his thing. After congratulating him on a job well done, I did a few card effects myself.

Next thing I knew, I was no longer at the bar. I was now sitting at a table in the corner of the room with about fifty people crowded around as I continued the pasteboard madness. Some people were sitting around the table, some were directly next to me, while most were standing. After numerous card bits, I decided to switch gears and grab the salt shaker setting to my right. I proceeded to make hand fulls of salt vanish and appear to the delight of the beer guzzling crowd. After the last production of salt, the man sitting straight across from me was burning the hell out of my right hand (*containing the gimmick*) and so, I *secretly* ditched the gimmick into my lap.

He had no idea. With my right hand, I reached over and picked up my beer to take a drink. Inside my head, I screamed, *"Touché,"* as I saw the man's shoulders slump. He realized there was actually nothing in my hand. Then I noticed, that the woman seated directly to my left had the strangest look on her face. She appeared **SHOCKED**. I followed where she was glaring at, and I realized she had a direct sight line into my lap.

By now, everyone reading this knows, I was using a THUMB TIP gimmick. Here's what it is. *Its a gimmick that looks exactly like a real thumb — flesh colored and all.*

So why was this woman shocked? Well, the THUMB TIP fell into the perfect position on my lap which made it appear as if I was *exposed*. It was standing straight up! I immediately understood her distress. You see, I was equally as upset, but not because she discovered my secret, but because I was not using a King-Size THUMB TIP. ♦

EXPOSED

P AN EXPENSIVE ARTY

Ivan Amodei

As Told by Ivan Amodei

The Gig: A posh event on the south side of Beverly Hills. A quick pop in at my client's Bel Air mansion to entertain a few out of town guests, and then off for the night's festivities in town. I entered the home and the client's son (*shaggy hair, skeleton tee shirt, underwear hanging out the top of his skater shorts*) greeted me with a grunt, as it appeared his hands were glued to the video game he was hypnotically intrenched by.

I set my bag down and went to greet the host. I went back to my car for a few extra things, and when I returned my bag had disappeared! I looked around and then a young boy came up to me and said, *"I know who took it."* He led me to a bedroom where a group of boys were playing video games. Pointing to the client's son in the room, he said, *"He took it!"* The accused immediately yelled, *"Yeah, I took it, and you're not getting it back!"* I considered hanging

ARE YOU KIDDING?

him by his toe nails until he talked, but I decided to find the person responsible for his parental guidance. I found his mother. She asked me, *"What would you like me to do?"* I suggested she speak with her son and demand that he return my belongings. With apprehension, she agreed. With mild force she requested the bag be returned. The monster she raised, did not look up from his game and arrogantly shouted, *"I'm not giving the bag back and leave me alone."* I was stunned. I thought we could tie him up and teach him what the *"D"* in discipline meant. But it was painfully clear the only *"D"* in this house represented — dysfunction.

I explained I would have to charge her for my full evening's fee, the rare Italian leather hand-stitched bag, its contents and everything else I could throw in to make it painful for her. She then approached the adolescent creature for the last time. **The conclusion:** I left that night with a luxurious check nestled in my pocket and a smile on my face.

My fee for not doing a single thing that night. Well, I'll let you guess, but whatever your estimate is — triple it. ◆

OUT
A KNOCK
ANDERS MODEN

AS TOLD BY ANDERS MODEN

I got a really funny letter from a young boy. It was from a beginner in magic who had bought HEALED & SEALED and wanted to tell me something. For those of you that do not know, I am the creator of this effect.

Briefly, David Blaine did the effect on one of his TV specials. It has become very popular for many to perform.

Here's the effect: A old, empty, and crushed soda can is magically restored to its original state right in front of your very eyes. To verify it, the magician pulls back on the tab to an audible *"pssst"* in fact, proving its new condition. Its an amazing effect and always gets great reactions.

Here is his letter he wrote just a few weeks after he performed my effect on a bunch of his friends at baseball practise.

Apparently, in this one instance, the reaction went a bit over the top.

I'm glad that his friend enjoyed the trick, but to go as far as he did, well, I don't know what he was thinking at the time. ♦

> Hi Anders,
>
> I'm sorry I did not answer your email sooner, but I was in the hospital. I performed your effect Healed and Sealed after baseball practice, and one of the guys freaked out so much, he hit me in the head with the baseball bat. I fell unconscious to the ground.
>
> Anyway, I'm much better now, and don't get me wrong, I'm not trying to blame you for this... LOL. I love the reactions I get, but the next time I perform Healed and Sealed, I'm going to wear a helmet.
>
> Just one more question? Do you have any more effects I could get from you? I'd love to do em.

CRAMPED

TIM ELLIS

AS TOLD BY TIM ELLIS

Back in 1981, I toured the Northern Territory (*the outback*) with a magic show for schools. A lot of these schools were in remote areas and very small, in fact, one school we performed our show in was in a caravan (*a vehicle equipped for living in and typically towed by a car*).

Try to imagine the scene, climbing up on top of the SUB-TRUNK, but staying crouched because your head is already hitting the roof. Lifting the cloth and holding it pressed firmly against the ceiling while you do the illusion.

The small audience was sure that we put a trapdoor in the roof of their caravan. Later, we had to fly to some remote mission stations in Arnhem Land at the top of the Northern Territory. Four of us, plus the illusions, crammed into a plane with only four seats. They had to remove one of the seats just to stuff all of the equipment in. I traveled laying down inside the ZIGZAG illusion the whole way. So, the next time you don't get the business-class seats you requested, don't complain, it could be a lot worse! ♦

QUICK BITS

There was only one performing magician in *The Magic Castle's Close-up Gallery* and one in the *Haunted Wine Cellar.* And almost every night there was a game of Hearts going on in the library upstairs. Invariably there would be Dai Vernon, Kuda Bux, Howard Hamburg, myself and a few others at various times, playing for fun.

Kuda Bux was originally from Pakistan and performed the best blindfold act I have ever seen. He loved to play cards, but occasionally he would renege unintentionally. I remember one night he reneged in following suit and everybody spotted it. Dai said, *"Kuda, why don't you put on your damned blindfold so you can see what you're doing!"*

— Ron Wilson

chapter
seven

Magic Fingers, tight spaces, cups, pennies, mentalism, lost luggage, nails, bosses

HIGH STAKES

R. PAUL WILSON

AS TOLD BY R. PAUL WILSON

The question you have to ask yourself is: **Do I want to go to jail for that?** There was an incredibly tempting job offer in Korea, but I knew better than to discuss it with my better half being its dangerous nature. Instead, on a trip to Vegas, I sat down with a friend and explained the proposition. I had a mate back in Glasgow that was very successful at Roulette. He had developed a powerful system to beat the game using a *new* technology that most of us now consider to be commonplace.

He had a good shot at **beating** a big Baccarat game in Korea with one of his business partners. There was however, a serious problem. The dealers were *"friendly"* to my mate's partner and would make sure the shuffle was easy to track. They had also been picking up the cards in order before placing them into the discard. This meant that the computer could record and keep track of the cards and always calculate the best outcome for the game. A large, *new* casino had thrown a wrench into the system. Their staff was ordered to scoop up the cards quickly, in one action, before hitting the discard. This could

DO I WANT TO GO TO JAIL FOR THAT?

I'D BE RICH, FAMOUS OR DEAD.

for every pickup with my solution. My mate liked the idea and, after sending it to his partner, I was offered a spot at the table. There would be a lot of money at stake, and I was up for a decent piece of that pie.

I was sitting across from my friend in Vegas, and I remember he leaned in and whispered to me, *"The question you have to ask yourself is — do I want to go to jail for that?"* I called my mate from the hotel and excused myself from the setup. The Korean system worked like a charm and made a ton of money, but I have no regrets.

I'm much happier understanding the ***world of cheating*** than I would be living in it. As I once told a journalist, *"If I really had the larceny to use the skills I've learned over the years, I'd be rich, famous or dead."*

Probably all three. ♦

result in the cards being mixed and their order impossible to determine now. My mate needed a solution and, after a few days, I hit on the perfect answer. The dealers could obey the *new* procedures, but almost guarantee a known outcome

A BAD PENNY

Shawn McMaster

As Told by Shawn McMaster

It was in 1990, and I was two years away from making magic my full-time profession. I had been performing for private parties and a few corporate gigs for a number of years and making fairly decent money, but the *"final leap,"* as it were, was still a couple of years down the road.

The fact that I wasn't a full-time pro, however, did not stop me from jumping into this wild profession head-long and doing everything that I thought it should entail. That included producing a few shows of my own.

The previous year, I had created and produced a comedy magic show called, I Can't Make Your Wife Beautiful and I Don't Vanish Statues (this was shortly after David Copperfield's now infamous *"Vanishing of the Statue of Liberty"* illusion). It was a *one-nighter* and the performance was sold out. Based on that success, the theater asked for another production the next year, and I was happy to oblige.

Flushed with my past success, I wanted to make this next show even better than the first, and with the help of my friend Keith Dion — a very talented and funny comedian who had actually opened for me in the first production — we set out to write a show that would showcase all of our talents (*ah, the enthusiasm of youth*). In my mind, this would also have to include some new magic material.

Many months previous to this, I had stumbled upon a little monograph written by Joe Karson (*the inventor of The Zombie*) in 1948 for a routine of his called *"The World's Fastest Card Trick."* Unimpressive in looks, this 10-page booklet offered to me what I thought would be a perfect addition to my act, and has continued to be one of my favorite pieces to perform even almost 20 years later. I changed the presentation quite a bit to fit my performance style, and wrote many new jokes, but I kept the basic concept the same due to the comedy potential inherent in the routine. I decided that this would be one of the routines I would perform in the new show.

I rehearsed it for a few months. The problem with rehearsing a routine like this, however, is that so much of the comedy relies on your interaction with the volunteer, and, therefore, your rehearsal tends to be a bit *"one-sided."*

Why does this always have to happen to me?

THE WORLD'S FASTEST CARD TRICK

You can practice and practice until you're exhausted, but in the end, the success or failure of the finished product relies on how the volunteer you bring up on-stage responds to the actions that are playing out, and how you can or can't respond to them. You can go in feeling confident in knowing every step of the journey, but one unexpected left turn by your volunteer can cause you to take detours that result in you ending up in unfamiliar and strange destinations that you had never intended to visit. Such was the case when I stepped out on that stage on November 15th, 1990 eager to share what I was sure would be a wonderfully funny new piece with my audience. There is always a sense of nervousness attributed to the debut of a new performance piece, but your confidence that it will all go as planned is in direct proportion to the amount of rehearsal and planning that goes into that piece. I had rehearsed a lot. It was the planning that, perhaps, I should have spent some more time on. There have been many times when, re-watching the recording of this performance from so many years ago, that I shout out to my own image to pick somebody else when I see myself scanning the audience at the beginning of the routine. But as expected, my recorded figure always picks the same woman, and up she walks to join me on-stage.

Penny.

Now, for those of you not familiar with Karson's original routine, the concept behind the comedy in *"The World's Fastest Card Trick"* is that the magician announces that he, with the help of his volunteer, will perform for the onlookers *"the world's fastest card trick."* The magician gives his volunteer a quick set of instructions that the volunteer is supposed to follow to make this card trick the quickest in the land, but because of the way the instructions are given, if they are followed exactly, a series of missteps occur within the routine. Missteps that appear to the audience, and the volunteer herself, as if they are mistakes, but in reality are exactly what the magician secretly wants. These *"mistakes"* cause the *"world's fastest card trick"* to drag on and on, and the comedy builds with

of solid comedy, with a magical card location at the end to boot.

Penny joined me on-stage and I confidently launched into the routine. I gave her the instructions, which during the first phase of this trick include, *"Take out any card and immediately sandwich it between your palms, keeping it face down at all times. Do not let anyone see the card for any reason whatsoever."* If those instructions, which I have since

the card, never having known its identity — leading to our first *"mistake"* when I quickly and triumphantly pluck *"her chosen card"* from out of the deck and ask her to announce the name of the card she picked only to sheepishly look at her when she states that she never looked at the card.

Well, at least that's how it was supposed to go.

Penny had followed my instructions to the point where I asked her to put the card back into the deck. As she moved to carry these new directions out, she flipped the card upright towards her so she could quickly glimpse the card's identity, then slid it back into the middle of the deck. Luckily, I saw her do it. Unluckily, I was now only 30 seconds into a planned seven-minute routine, and all seven minutes had now been flushed down the toilet due to her

IT DRAGS ON AND ON AND ON

each successive *"miscommunication."* Depending on how the volunteer I pick reacts to what is going on within the trick, this routine runs between seven to eight minutes. Seven to eight minutes

adjusted a little, were followed exactly, Penny would have chosen a card and sandwiched it in her hands without looking at it. Following my further instructions, she would have replaced

That's how it was supposed to go?

DO NOT LET A
ANYONE SEE THE CARD FOR
ANY REASON WHATSOEVER

seeing what the card was. How could a routine that depends on the volunteer not knowing the identity of her card continue when she knew the card she picked? I hadn't planned for that. My mind reeled. In the span of about four seconds it went through every possible contingency of how I could salvage the routine and still make it enjoyable to watch. I resolved to control the card to the top, palm it off, and produce it from my wallet in my inside coat pocket.

Granted it wouldn't be very impressive, and it was far from what I had planned to do, but at least it would end somewhat magically. It would truly end up being *"the world's fastest card trick"* and the audience would have no way of knowing what they missed. I began to execute my plan. I plucked out a card and triumphantly showed it to the audience, asking Penny to name the card she had just picked. Of course, the card she named was not the one I was holding. I feigned surprise, palmed off the real chosen card from the top as I had a few words of byplay with Penny, then handed her the deck and said, *"I give up, you find it!"* As Penny took the deck, I casually put both hands into my pants pockets figuring the card could hide there as she searched through the deck. Penny never even began the search. *"It's not in the deck,"* she said matter-of-factly. *"Excuse me?" "It's not in the deck,"* she repeated the words that shot ice water through my veins. *"You took it out of the deck."* A sneaking suspicion arose in my mind. *"Penny, are you a magician?"* I asked. *"No,"* she said, *"but I know a little about magic, and I know that when you handed me the deck, you somehow had a hold on my card, and you slid it out something like this."* She attempted to demonstrate a palm that curled and crushed one of the cards from my deck as she continued her explanation, *"Usually, the eyes follow the hand, and when you handed me the deck you slipped the card out. Everybody's eyes followed your hand with the deck and watched me take it, and you stuck the card into your pocket."*

I really hadn't planned for that. What could I do? She had me dead to rights. And despite the atrocious nature of her demonstration of a palm, her explanation was nothing short of an impromptu lecture on the elements of misdirection.

I REALLY HADN'T PLANNED FOR THAT

WELL, I GUESS THE TRICKS OVER!

A lecture she had decided to deliver onstage to me and a theatre full of people! Stunned, I thought there was nothing I could do now, but to own up to the fact that she was correct. I reached into my pants pocket, extracted her card, tore it into tiny pieces and said, *"Well, I guess that trick's over!"*

As I tossed the pieces into the air. I excused Penny back to her seat, and the show moved on without incident. Every chance we got, however, Keith and I would joke about Penny in countless call-backs that we peppered throughout the rest of the performance. The final surprise occurred after the show had ended and people were filing out the front door. Keith and I were in the lobby greeting people and thanking them for coming. Many of the guests said to me as they were leaving how funny they had thought my *"plant in the audience"* had been.

They thought the whole thing had been planned, and I decided to leave it that way. One last bit of information that should be mentioned here. As we found out that night when Penny entered the lobby to leave along with everyone else, the reason she was hip to magic techniques was that she was dating a magician, with whom she had attended that night's show.

Lucky me. I don't know that I ever got his name, but it didn't matter. The name *"Penny"* was enough for me to remember, and believe me, I haven't forgotten it after all these years. ♦

CUP OF DOOM

GERRY KATZMAN

As Told by Gerry Katzman

I was street-performing at the Los Feliz Street Fair in Los Angeles. As I neared the end of my act, I noticed, out of the corner of my eye, a mylar balloon, that had come free from a balloon stand, floating slowly up toward the sky. My street act was going really, really well.

I had a huge receptive audience gathered, laughing at everything I said, I felt really *"in the zone"* as I started my last trick, the CHOP CUP, which was a beautiful metal cup and a ball effect.

The routine had a generic intro, something like: *"Ladies and Gentlemen, behold the Cup of Doom!"* For some reason, at this moment, a big biker guy, in the front row decided

TRYING TO RECOVER CONTROL

that he didn't like my show, and in the most mocking tone bellowed, *"Why is it called the Cup of Doom?"* The way he said it was filled with such animosity toward me, and I admit, it side-tracked me for a second. I had no reply and

the audience sensed it. You know, as a performer, the feeling of losing the crowd. It's an out of control sensation, and sometimes, the only thing you can think of to do is continue with the show.

I neared the end of the first phase of the routine. It's where the cup is slammed onto the table and vanishes.

I noticed the silver balloon, speeding quickly across the sky, toward the power station that gives electricity to most of Eastern Los Angeles.

Trying to recover control, I launched into the finale of the trick. Holding the CHOP CUP in my right hand, my arm swung it in an upwards arc, high into the air.

As I started to being it down fast toward the table, I saw the silver balloon float directly into the housing of the power transformer. As the rim of the cup made hard contact with the wood

table, I heard and felt the largest sonic boom rip through me, as the power station that brings electricity to one of the largest cities in the United States got *short-circuited* by a balloon.

Everything that was powered by electricity stopped. The music, the games, the carousel, the lights, ALL became a vacuum of stunned silence. The audience stared at me in shock. They had no idea what had just happened and were looking to me for answers. I took a deep breath, smiled, and said, *"That's why it's called the Cup of Doom!"* The big biker guy had nothing else to say. ◆

Did You Know?

Erich Weiss (HOUDINI)
March 24, 1874 — October 31, 1926

Houdini did not die while performing his WATER TORTURE CELL illusion, but died of peritonitis from a ruptured appendix (*the same condition that killed Rudolph Valentino*).

M GOING ENTAL

ERIC DECAMPS

AS TOLD BY ERIC DECAMPS

I know I'm dating myself, but back in the late 1970s, I had a particular experience with a mental magic piece that scarred me from doing any mentalism for long time.

HIS HIGH SCHOOL MAGIC CLUB

I was in my first year of college, and I was doing my magician's apprenticeship at New York's Magic Towne House. At the Towne House, I had become friends with another young magician named Ray Nordini. Ray was a senior in high school at the time and the president of his school's magic club. His high school magic club would produce an annual magic show. This year, Ray had organized a comedy magic act, a manipulation act, an illusion act, a general magic act and an escape act. Ray approached me and asked if I would do a mentalism piece for the show and I reluctantly agreed. I was new to magic, but thought to myself, I'll just go through some of the mentalism stuff I had and see what I could concoct. In my magic drawer I found the then marketed trick, RANDOMENTAL created by Richard Stride. For those not familiar with this piece, about 150 old punched out computer data processing cards are used. Each card has a different random four digit number on it. These random numbered cards were originally used back in the 50s, 60s and 70s by polltakers to obtain statistically unbiased selections in connection with public opinion polls.

Three people freely select cards and randomly call out the digits from their cards. Four random three digit numbers are created and added together for a total. The total, a different one every time you perform it, matches a prediction that you have made way ahead of time. It's very clean, fair looking and astonishing when done correctly. The operative word here is, CORRECTLY!

Let me set the stage. The auditorium is packed with over 500 people. I am introduced and the curtains open revealing two giant classroom black boards on-stage. One of which has a big sheet covering my prediction. The other is set to write the random numbers

picture. It's the day of the show. I have more confidence than when the mighty Casey, from Ernest Lawrence Thayer's famous Poem, stepped up to bat. I'm going to knock this out of the park, a grand slam. I'm going to be the hit of the show. Let me add some color to this

Tony Manero wannabe mentalist was large and in charge. All kidding aside, I'm doing fantastic. The audience is in the palm of my hands. They are buying my presentation and my audience management is spectacular. Well I thought my audience management was spectacular until the random numbers were totaled. To my surprise the total on the board didn't match my covered prediction.

Thinking it was a math error, I scurried over to the board and took the chalk away from the audience member who was doing the arithmetic. What an idiot I thought, she obviously can't add! However, me being the Disco Dunniger could easily sum up the numbers correctly. I added and came up with the same total she did. I tried again, same total. I must have missed something and added again and got the same total.

THE OPERATIVE WORD HERE IS CORRECTLY!

that are to be called out. Mind you, all week during the rehearsals, I have been nailing this thing 100% of the time. I have the director, the cast and crew all amazed because every time they see it, a totally new number is arrived to and my prediction always matched that random total. As far as they were concerned, I was one step away from starting my own religion. Now let me set the

picture. It's the late 1970s and the film, *Saturday Night Fever* is all the rage. I'm all dressed in my white suit and open collared black shirt. In my mind, I was the Hispanic Tony Manero ready to do some mentalism. In other words, the Disco Dunninger. And just like disco, this concept went down in flames!

The introduction went exactly as planned the stage looked great and the

I hate MATH!

TONIGHT, I HAVE TRIED AND FAILED.

Sweat was now covering my brow. My week of rehearsals flashed through my minds eye. During all those rehearsals I was a star and here on my night, the night that I would shine, the night that this boy would be crowned king of all mentalism. I was sadly reduced to a lowly court jester.

I summand whatever pride I had left turned to the audience and said, *"This Ladies and Gentlemen was an experiment of the mind. And like most experiments that probe into the unknown, they do not always work. Tonight I have tried and failed."* As I headed off stage, I walked by the covered blackboard grabbed a corner of the sheet and dramatically revealed my incorrect prediction. The curtains closed and I was done.

Here's what happened. One of the audience members didn't understand English very well and when I had asked her to call out random digits for the card she was holding she misunderstood what I said and called whatever random digits that came to her mind. Now if the piece worked that way it would have been awesome, but it didn't and it wasn't. The valuable lesson I learned is to make sure that ALL instructions you give audience members are VERY clear and precise.

Double check and even triple check to make sure that the audience members you have chosen understand exactly what you want them and need them to do. It's not their fault. It's your fault for not making sure they understand what you need them to do.

If you follow this advice maybe when you go to reveal your prediction you will not have hear an auditorium full of people shout, *"That the mighty Disco Dunniger has just struck out!"* ♦

chapter
eight

Contests, teachers, luggage, Los Angeles, weird meetings, card tricks, corporate executives, fires, celebrities, bathrooms, car problems and more

NOSE
UNDER YOUR

DANNY COLE

AS TOLD BY DANNY COLE

I was booked for a very important show in Madrid, Spain. When I arrived at the airport, the two cases holding my equipment did not show up at baggage claim. Big surprise. Airline agents couldn't tell me where they were either. After a few hours passed, I began getting worried.

Of course, airport personnel tried to assure me the bags would probably arrive soon and that I should not worry. They gave me a hotline to call to check in on things. I did call, and call, and call, and of course, the answer each time, *"No bags have arrived."*

Frustrated, I went back to the airport because I thought I could get some answers in person. After all, I had a show soon and I needed my act! The agent told me that my bags were lost

> ## HUNDREDS OF BAGS OF EVERY SHAPE AND SIZE.

and probably still in Los Angeles. *"Great,"* I said. *"That's just perfect."* They advised me to go back to my hotel and keep calling the hotline. On a whim, I decided to go down to the baggage claim area and have a look around.

I asked a nearby agent if they knew anything about my gear. They said, *"No,"* but offered to let me check the storage area. They led me to a locked door that opened into a gigantic room lined to the roof with suitcases and luggage and everything else you could imagine people travel with. Hundreds of bags of every shape and size were

stuffed into that room. I thought, *"Well, I'm screwed. It's going to be like finding a needle in a haystack."* I collapsed on a piece of luggage with my head hung low. I thought, *"How am I going to find my bags in this mess? This really stinks."* My hands clasped over my face, I rubbed my eyes in disbelief.

I have to look through each and every aisle, top to bottom. Then, as my eyes came into focus, I saw out of the corner of my eye, my **tag** from my bag. I was sitting on it all along! What? Right in front of me — there they were!

Now that's magic. ♦

A FINAL BOW

TOMMY COOPER

As Told by Ivan Amodei

> ## ONE OF THE FUNNIEST GUYS YOU'VE EVER SEEN!

Tommy Cooper was a famous British comedian/magician and one of the funniest guys you've ever seen. A towering man and English gentlemen. For years, Tommy was the star of his own TV show, *"The Tommy Cooper Hour."* Also known as the *fez-wearing* magician whose tricks always seemed to go wrong.

What happened to him on April 15, 1984 goes down as a tremendous tragedy in entertainment history.

In Britain, he was making a rare TV appearance, as one of the acts on *"Live From Her Majesty's."* Tommy was doing his act and people were having a great time. If you have seen Tommy's act or even bits and pieces, you understood that he seldom got through one full effect. But because he was so comedically brilliant, he could pick up a rock and make it funny. So whatever happened on-stage, whether disastrous or not, the audience always knew Tommy was in control.

During one funny bit, Tommy was wearing a long robe/cloak down to the ground. He is also nearly touching the stage's *back-curtain*.

He magically began to remove the most unusual and funny props from within his cloak, such as mannequin legs, long poles and even large ladders. Everyone was hysterically laughing, but also fully aware that someone was feeding him these props from behind the curtain. All of a sudden, Tommy leaned back against the curtain a bit more forcefully than usual, and collapsed to the floor. The live audience continued laughing and thought this was just another clumsy bit Tommy was doing.

No one knew, not the live spectators, the TV audience, stage crew or friends that Tommy had a *heart-attack* at that exact moment. And only ten minutes after his collapse at 8:40pm, Tommy Cooper died. It was an incident that stunned his fans, Great Britain and the world of entertainment.

He is greatly missed. ♦
(1921–1984)

THE SET-UP

IVAN AMODEI

AS TOLD BY IVAN AMODEI

I never leave home to go do a show without eating something. You never know if you are going to have a chance to eat at the show, so better to be safe than grumpy.

I was on my way to the Comedy Magic Club in Hermosa Beach, CA. It's a 90-minute drive out there from my home. I decided I should eat, but was running late and with traffic, I thought the best way was to eat in my car. All loaded up with food, drinks and gas I am on my way. About 90 minutes went by and I still had not arrived. Traffic is the worst in Los Angeles, especially

CAN I PLEASE USE YOUR BATHROOM?

WHAT THE HELL IS GOING ON IN THIS CITY?

on a Friday night. Now it hit me, I gotta go to the bathroom very badly. I thought, *"Well maybe I can wait it out and go when I get to the club."* But after looking up ahead at the traffic and the mess that was up there, I decided I had better exit and find a place quick.

Shortly after, I found a gas station. I ran inside and asked the clerk, *"Can I please use your restroom?"* The attendant quickly replied, *"NO!"* I said, *"I'll buy something, I really have to go."* Another abrupt, *"NO!"* Instead of arguing with him, I looked around and

saw a burger joint across the street. I quickly ran over there. The owner was greeting guests as they walked into the store. I said, *"Hello, can I please use your bathroom?"* He belts out, *"NO!"* I thought, *"What the hell is going on in this city?"* I really have to go bad, so I said, *"But I plan on eating, I just have to use the bathroom first."* He replied, *"Oh, if you eat then you can use the bathroom."* Finally at last. Now, I'm not even hungry. I didn't care what I ordered, but I slapped $5.00 down for a burger solely to use the bathroom.

When I came out of the restroom, the owner was standing there with a deck of cards in his hands. I'm thought, *"Umm, did my deck fall out of my pocket in my rush past him?"* I checked and I still had my deck. He said to me, *"While you are waiting for your food, would you like to see a card trick."* I thought, *"Wow, this is weird."* I replied, *"Okay, sure."* He showed me his card trick and then asked, *"How did you like it?"* I said, *"It was alright."* He quickly replied, *"Alright? All my customers I show this to love it."* I said, *"I understand,*

but it was alright." He said, *"Why just alright?"* I answered, *"Because you are not using full deck."*

He answered, *"No, this IS a full deck."* So I said, *"Let me see the cards then."* I immediately said, *"You see, you do not have a full deck here, let me show you."* I quickly pulled down my pant's zipper and removed the card he had me select. The look on his face and the face of his friend (*I think a manager*) was unreal.

Complete and total shock! Like they were just hit by a MAC Truck going 100mph. Then he rattled off a bunch of phrases and sentences in his native language, which I think was Persian.

Maybe he ordered a hit on me, I don't know. I figured, I'd better get the heck out of there fast. This guy was pissed.

Finally, the guy behind the counter said, *"Number three, your order is ready."* I said, *"Okay, great thanks!"*

The owner then said to me, *"Get the hell out of my store now."* I replied, *"But what about my burger?"* He yelled, *"No burger, get the hell out now!"*

I quickly left the store with no food in hand, and just paid $5.00 to go to the bathroom.

One thing I do have to say, *"You gotta love LA!"* ♦

LIKE THEY WERE HIT BY A MAC TRUCK!

THE CONTEST

CHRIS RANDALL

AS TOLD BY CHRIS RANDALL

Some of my worst shows will not seem that bad to most people. To the uninitiated, lighting my hand on fire during a show or pressing a button for a pyro cue that would eminently burn my friend's face, might sound terrible. But it's not. Having a LOSANDER FLOATING TABLE fly off into the front row and break into

PRODUCTION OF A DEAD DOVE

pieces, all while Losander is in the audience, might sound humiliating, but it's not. Lit candles falling out from underneath my coat, and the production of a dead dove might seem horrifying. But it's not. Especially when you compare the above to the 2008 World Magic Seminar Gold Lion's Head Competition fiasco. Before my story unfolds, you must understand that winning this competition has been my long-term goal and lifelong dream.

I grew up in Las Vegas Nevada, the long-time home of the WMS. Every year, I'd sneak into the convention with my friends and watch the best acts in the world compete for the Gold Lion's Head. It was while watching these contests that I knew one day I would be the United States representative, and win that honorary title.

My heroes James Dimmare, Rocco, and Jason Byrne were all gold winners. In later years, new and amazing acts like Lee Eun Gyeol, Florian Zimmer, and Kenji Minemura earned the coveted title. I knew it would one day be my turn. I was of the impression that it was my birthright!

After many years of dreaming and planning, I started competing in random magic competitions in my early twenties. Eventually, I tried my act out at one of the International Brotherhood of Magicians stage contest, but never won (*or even made the finals*).

After three valiant attempts competing at the I.B.M., traveling the world, and a few trips to The Magic

How much more could I possibly practise?

IT WAS A DISASTER

Castle, I finally felt the act was strong enough to submit my application video for the World Magic Seminar. To my amazement, I was chosen to represent the U.S. I practiced and rehearsed for months, performing free shows whenever I could. I also spent a lot of time, mentally and physically preparing. I thought through everything that could go wrong, and arranged a course of action for those instances.

I even snuck into the Orleans' Theater (*where the competition would be held*), days before the contest, and became friendly with the stage crew. They allowed me to spend time in the lights, on-stage, so I could get *"comfortable."*

Primed and ready to win this competition, I felt I had done everything to prepare for the biggest day of my life. For 15 years, I had dreamt of this moment, and now this was my opportunity to achieve my dream. It was my time. The night before, I made extra cue sheets for the tech rehearsal, practiced several more times, and loaded the car. You bet I was careful to check to make sure all parts of the act were accounted for, and present.

After a good night's sleep, I woke up early so I could enjoy my big day. Upon my arrival to the Orleans Hotel and Casino, I felt great loading in my act, picking a dressing room, and preparing for the tech rehearsal. One of the memories that sticks in my head

to this day is the stage manager being very aggressive and short with all the competitors. I watched him spend most of his time screaming at Jorgos from Greece. In hindsight, he never gave attention to either me or Sterling Dietz during this tech time. It did not matter, or so I thought.

I felt my tech cues were simple: *lights on, open curtain, blackout at the end*.

This specific competition had consumed my life for a long time, and now all I had to do was perform.

One of the best memories I have is of all the people in the crowd that were there to support me. My girlfriend at the time, close friends from all over the world who hadn't seen me perform in years, most every magician I had assisted in my youth, and the man I wanted to see me win the most was in attendance — my father.

The first two acts went on with less-than-overwhelming responses from the crowd. I was on third, and felt good. Standing in the wings waiting, I ran through the act in my head one last time: *fire to ball, ball to smoke, ball split, billiard balls*. I heard my name announced, and walked on-stage. I was ready. The music started, the curtain opened. The fire was lit, it changed to the ball, and as the ball was heading to the ground, I realized at that exact moment that the stage and spot lights were not on at all. The stage manager had missed his one single cue!

Jolting in the dark to catch the ball, I moved off my mark and grabbed the round piece of rubber. Luckily, I found it. However, this sudden movement dislodged my next ball for the split, causing it and a shell to tumble to the stage floor. It was in that instant that the stage lights came up. There I was, with one ball in hand and the other pieces lost on the floor. This was something I did not plan for! There's nothing you can do to prepare for everything. Some things just happen.

I quickly vanished the ball to a puff of smoke, and then reproduced it. All the while, watching my fellow competitors point to the missing parts from the wings. I picked up the other ball and shell. I looked to the audience knowing I had lost my dream in that moment, and proceeded to do the rest of my act as best I could.

All the while in my head, all I could think was that my act is great when the lights are on! To add insult to injury, as I hit the final pose of my act, I noticed that the curtain had closed on my confetti launcher. It was an amazing display of flying paper, it's just too bad only the stage hands and other competitors were the only ones to see it. I walked off stage, and had to fight hard to quiet my emotions. Anger, disappointment, and tears overwhelmed me once I was alone in the dressing room.

While the host, friends, and the convention organizers offered many apologies for the cues missed by their stage manager, I was devastated. I had done all I could to ready myself for the moment. What took six months to prepare for, took only seconds to destroy.

That day would haunt me for years to come. Nonetheless, there's a silver lining to this gray cloud. It's this specific instance which inspired me to make the opening of my act even easier, and more important, to always wait to see the lights go on before I ever set foot on the stage. ♦

SLOWLY MY BAG BEGAN TO EMIT SMALL WISPS OF SMOKE AS I CONTINUED WITH THE ACT. AS THE VOLUME OF SMOKE BEGAN TO INCREASE, THE OTHER ACTOR IN THE SHOW TRIED TO GET MY ATTENTION BY POINTING AT MY BAG.

WHEN I DIDN'T NOTICE, HE ACTUALLY CAME UP AND UNDER HIS BREATH SAID, "YOUR BAG IS ON FIRE!"

— A HOT ACT *page 113*

THANK YOU MAESTRO

TONY SLYDINI

AS TOLD BY TONY BINARELLI

During my wanderings through the magical world of illusion, I have had the opportunity to meet some extraordinary people, who have deeply affected my performance routines and artistic development, but above all, have helped me mature as a human being. One of these is unquestionably Tony Slydini.

We met for the first time near Vienna, at the Austrian Magic Convention, where I had accompanied a good friend of mine, Giampaolo Zelli, a prominent Italian surgeon and prestidigitation enthusiast, who, had he undertaken a career in the field of magic instead of medicine, would have been equally successful.

Slydini was one of the attractions at the convention, if not the number one star, and would always be surrounded by the organizers and a large crowd of fans, which made it quite difficult to approach him. But luck or, more likely, the empathy stimulated by my great desire to meet him, would come to my aid. I was sitting by myself at a table in the dining room when his vivid sparkling eyes crossed mine and, I don't know how, nor why, but this little great man left the crowd surrounding him, crossed the room and came to sit opposite me. In his typical Italian-American accent, and with a hint of the dialect of Foggia he said, *"You're Italian, I can sense it."* It reminded me of an Italian-American character from Brooklyn in a film by Scorsese.

He continued, *"Did you know I was born near Foggia, in 1901, and my father was an amateur conjuror? It was he who passed on to me his passion for sleight of hand. Unfortunately, there was nothing for us to do in Italy, so my family moved first to Argentina, where I*

THAT'S WHERE THE DOLLARS ARE!

A DOLLAR MAGICALLY APPEARED

started working as an illusionist in the vaudeville theatres until 1929. When the depression came, and in 1930, I decided to move to New York. The United States is the place for opportunity, I thought to myself. That's where the dollars are! It'll certainly bring me good luck." As he said, *"Where the dollars are,"* a dollar bill magically appeared in his hand. He autographed it and gave it to me. In fact, it wasn't the one dollar bill that brought me luck that day, but Tony Slydini himself. Some time after our meeting and having been invited by Zelli, Syldini visited Italy for the first time. I was given the chance to become a pupil of Slydini, together with a small group of Roman conjuring enthusiasts. We all profited enormously from this demanding and great teacher.

It's thanks to him that I won the second prize in card magic at the World Championships. Concerning this prize, I have a rather curious story to tell. I had been invited to take part in the Tannen Jubilee, one of the top magical events in America, in New Jersey, not far from New York. Of course, I stopped over in the Big Apple for a few days, attracted by the charm of the only city in the world that is not a city, but a world all its own. Moreover, having the opportunity to call on Tony Slydini, who lived on a small side street off Fifth Avenue, in one of those typical New York lofts with a small green door and narrow stairs. There was a huge lounge, with a kitchenette and a large round green table. Everywhere there were prizes, awards, plaques, photographs and pictures of the Virgin Mary and Mussolini, of great magicians and young pupils of his, even a light-up Venetian gondola next to a small brightly-painted Sicilian cart. Slydini welcomed me in and said, *"Come on in, I'll make you a plate of orecchiette alla foggiana, just like my mother used to*

make," and without offense to anybody else, they turned out to be the best I've ever eaten. While we were talking, after dinner, I mentioned to Slydini, without

When I finished, Slydini looked me directly in the eyes and said, *"And they even gave you a prize for that? You made no less than seven mistakes!"*

me, trying to correct my mistakes. I don't know whether I still make those mistakes, *maybe just a few*, but what I do know is that I still often perform the

SLYDINI LOOKED AT ME IN THE EYES

concealing the pride and gratitude I felt, the prize I had won thanks to the techniques he'd taught me in Rome, to which he said, *"I'm very pleased for you, let's see what you did."* I showed him my routines with a certain amount of apprehension, I must confess.

He gave me his trademark slap on the hands. I was surprised, and to be honest, rather miffed. I replied, *"Did I? Can you show me which ones?"* He took the cards and showed me the seven mistakes I had actually made, one by one. Slydini spent that whole day with

same routines and still get the better of many fellow magicians with them.

For which all I can say is, *"Thank you, Maestro!"* ♦

H A HOLE IN THE HEAD

TOM BURGOON

AS TOLD BY TOM BURGOON

I'm doing walk around magic during the cocktail hour of a no name airplane parts company in the middle of Iowa. My strolling time is complete and I'm getting ready to head upstairs to my hotel room to get rid of the close-up stuff and reload for the after dinner show.

Just as I started walking out the door, a man walked up to me and said, *"Can you do that trick again where you stick the half dollar on your forehead?"* I said, *"Sure."* The effect is the old bit, where you place a coin on your forehead and it sticks. Then you apparently reveal how its done and show the audience that you have a coin with a nail

Fred decided to get rid of his opening trick.

in it. A simple switch for the actual coin with a duplicate coin and a **nail** welded to it. I did the effect for him. He's now looking at the coin with the nail, but he doesn't laugh or react in any way. Suddenly he snatched the spiked coin from my hand and proceeded to smack himself in the forehead with it. He did it so quickly there was no way of stopping him. As his hand came away from his face he was still holding the spiked coin, but there was also a small trickle of blood coming from the center of his forehead. He said, *"You could hurt someone doing that!"* I said, *"YES, IF YOU STICK THAT IN YOUR HEAD!"* He's

A Hole in the Head!

now talking about a law suit and wiping the blood from his head. He stomped away to another part of the ball room. I, in the mean time, ran up to my room and called my lawyer. My lawyer assured me that everything would be OK.

I decided I should talk to the owners of the company about the incident. I had a micro cassette recorder and placed it into the breast pocket of my jacket. I wanted a recording of what they said to me. I talked to the President and Vice President, and a few others high up in the company, and they all said pretty much the same thing, *"That's OK, we don't like him anyway."*

I noticed that during the stand-up show the guy was laughing and having a good time. I don't do that effect any more. ♦

Did You Know?

Houdini held a patent for a style of diving suit. The innovation was granted U.S. Patent **Number 1,370,316** on March 1, 1921.

The improved construction of the suit was a direct result of Houdini's direct interest in underwater escapes.

THE PATENT READS:
"The invention relates to deep sea diving suits or armors, and its object is to provide a new and improved diver's suite arranged to permit the diver, in case of danger for any cause whatever, to quickly divest himself of the suit while being submerged and to safely escape and reach the surface of the water. Another object is to enable the diver to put on or take off the suit without requiring assistance."

THE BOSS

ASI WIND

AS TOLD BY ASI WIND

TIME IS MONEY. My routine where I make a spectator's bill disappear and reappear beneath their watch. It's really a powerful effect. During a walk around gig one night, I performed it on this one guy. He was so blown away by it that he wanted me to do it for his *big boss*. Obviously, due to the nature of the trick, watching it a second time gives the spectator quite an advantage. First, he knows where the bill is going to end up, and secondly, I do have to load the bill under the person's watch somehow. Although the conditions were not in my favor, I took the challenge and asked him to escort me to the big boss. As we made our way to find the boss, I asked the guy not to tell his boss anything about the trick since he knew what was going to happen. He of course said that there was no problem and that he would say nothing. I was introduced to the *"big boss,"* the president of the company, and asked him to remove the largest bill he had on him. What a surprise, it was a $100 bill. I started performing the

INTRODUCED TO THE "BIG BOSS"

effect, and I immediately saw the other guy watching the routine with a smile and probably thinking, *"I know exactly what's going to happen."*

After I made the bill vanish, I was just about to tell the *"big boss"* where the bill was. But I looked at the other guy and told him, *"Why don't you tell him where the bill is?"*

Enthusiastically he said, *"It's under your watch."* The boss looked under his wristwatch and found nothing. Then I looked at the other guy and asked him, *"Why do you think it's under his watch? It's actually under YOUR watch again."*

Since that time, I've tried to repeat this sequence again and again. It's funny how something so risky and unexpected turned into a great moment in my show on a consistent basis. I guess things happen for a reason. ♦

One of the magic fraternity's most respected magicians was Charles Miller. Charlie was a charming stage performer and appeared on my **It's Magic!**

Show back in the late sixties. As a card expert he was is that class that included Dai Vernon, Nate Leipzig, Max Malini and other legends in magic.

The younger magicians that were devotees of sleight of hand were often surprised and envious to see me with the great Charlie Miller and deep in conversation at the end of The Magic Castle bar.

Was he imparting the great secrets of magic or some new Charlie Miller move? No! Charlie loved to talk about the comedy and novelty acts in vaudeville.

But never about magic, moves, magicians or anything related to magic. It just frustrated all the younger magicians who thought that they would be insider secrets if they just listened in enough.

— Milt Larsen

FIRE
ALARM

PETER SAMELSON

AS TOLD BY PETER SAMELSON

I'm not sure how many of you know that I spent over 15 years working ships. Not full time, in the sense that I would sign up for a 9 to 12 month contract, but full-time in the way that I would book a two to three week run on a ship, then be home long enough to remember. I liked New York and then head off to do a series of college shows, or put together the pieces for a corporate or theater event. So life was hectic and rolling ahead at pace that only a steamroller could envy. It would take a lot to bring me up short, to make me take a moment to reflect.

The opening of the Cruise Act was very elegant, I wore the look of an impresario, Borsalino hat, long white neck scarf, outer coat slung on my shoulders over my tuxedo. Jeff McBride helped shape the opening moments as we played one day in his apartment on 52nd street. The white scarf comes off the neck, I blow a kiss to the prettiest woman in the front row, who tosses one back. The kiss appears on the scarf, then from there, a bouquet of flowers bursts forth. It was just before this moment that, one evening, time stood still.

Here is how it supposed to look. As I enter to my music, fire instantly appears in one hand, becomes a red silk, reappears from the silk and vanishes, as the silk becomes a cane. The hat rolls and spins happen just before they are set aside and the white scarf is pulled from around my neck. The fire reappears in the center of the scarf, and is picked up and tossed high in the air, above the audiences heads where it burst

ONE EVENING,
TIME STOOD STILL

ON THAT NIGHT, SOMETHING WENT WRONG

into a shower of sparks. On that night, something went wrong. I had clipped the little package of flash paper from beneath the bottom edge of my tux and touched the tip to the flame. My left hand immediately sent it skyward. It seemed the flash paper must have been very old, for as I watched in horror, it arced up, up, up over the heads of the audience whose faces were turned up to watch it. Up to the top of its trajectory, it burned and burned, and continued to *slowly* burn, heading back down to earth. Down, down, ever more slowly down. I'm not sure time actually stopped, but I could see each fraction of a second frozen in time as the burning coal headed down into the bouffant hair of a woman in the front row. I have to admit, I did not even have time to think *"hair product,"* before I was off the stage and patting the top of her head. And with my luck, her surprised lawyer husband said to me, *"I'll talk to you after the show."*

I'll never know exactly how the Cruise Line and I avoided being sued for every cent we had, but all I can think was maybe, in spite of everything, they liked the act. ♦

A CRAPPY
TRICK

TONY GIORGIO

AS TOLD BY HOWARD HAMBURG

IT WILL APPEAR IN ANY ROOM YOU WANT

Tony Giorgio is a world renowned card technician/actor and has appeared in many famous films, including *The Godfather*. He is very respected in the magic industry.

One night, at The Magic Castle, Tony and I were sitting at the bar directly in front of the Close-Up room. Tony was entertaining four women from the TV industry. He was doing card tricks for them. They had seen magic all day so finding a card or producing it from his pocket really didn't impress them much.

"We have to impress them," I thought. I whispered into Tony's ear, *"Go out with it, go out with it."* Which meant in secret magic language, we all speak, (*remove the card from the deck and secretly hold it in your hand*). Tony had her sign a card and replace it into the deck. Then he's *"out with it"* and the card is in his left hand, casually resting to his side. I secretly took the signed card from him. He asked her to shuffle the deck as he continued talking with them. I left with the card and went over to the women's bathroom and knocked on the door.

I didn't hear a response, so I went in and I placed the card on a toilet seat. I came back and whispered into Tony's ear while he was talking, *"Women's toilet seat."* I selected the one stall that you would see directly in front of you as you entered the bathroom. He told the lady who signed her card, *"Your card is gone!"* He said, *"It will appear in any room in this Castle that you would like it to appear. For instance, the Library, the Kitchen, the Woman's room and so forth."* She said, *"The Woman's room!"* He immediately replied, *"GO!"* And she said, *"What, where?"* He said, *"To the Woman's room."* Remember, he had not left the bar. She left for the woman's room and came out screaming, whiter than a ghost holding her signed card. She literally was shaking. She could not believe what had just happened. About six months to a year roughly pass and

A Crappy Trick

Tony and I are again sitting at the bar in front of the Close-Up room. This time, Larry Jennings is about six stools down from us. A guy with a nice looking girl came up to Tony and said, *"Tony this is my fiancé, and I would really appreciate it if you could just do something special for her. Would you please as a favor for me? Cause she has heard so much about you from me."*

Tony turned his head and looked at me. Never said a word to me, but I knew exactly what he was telling me. And I nodded in acknowledgment. Tony had this girl select a card and sign it. And once again *"out he goes with it"* just like some time ago. I again, secretly took the card from him, and headed for the Woman's room.

Because it was a busy Friday night, I was not able to enter the Woman's room. I asked a young lady magician friend of mine, *"Could you do me a favor and go into the Woman's bathroom and place this card on the woman's toilet seat. The first one you see when you walk in. Stick around because that woman in the blue dress over there is going to be steered into that room somehow."* She said, *"Sure, of course."*

When Tony got the tip that the card was once again on the toilet seat, he quickly went into the final part of the card trick sequence. He said, *"Your card is gone!"* He showed her all the cards. He continued, *"It will appear in any room in this Castle that you would like it to appear. For instance, the Library, the Kitchen, the Woman's Room and so forth. Where would you like it to be?"* She said, *"The Woman's Room."* He immediately replied, *"GO!"* She said, *"Go where?"* He answered, *"To the Woman's Room."* So off she went.

She came out screaming. I thought she was going to pass out. Her hands were trembling. She was holding her signed card completely amazed by what just happened. Larry Jennings, who was sitting only a few feet away chirped in and said, *"Hey what's going on here?"* Tony turned to him and said, *"The lady signed a card, I never left the bar, she picked the ladies room and the signed card was on the toilet seat."*

Larry SLAMMED his hand down on the bar and said *"GOD Damn it, that my trick!"* Just to clarify, Larry did a trick called *"Card to Urinal."*

When Tony wrote this story in Genii Magazine years ago he wrote, *"So we can keep magic history correct,* **Card to Urinal** *is Larry Jenning's trick and* **Card to Crapper** *is Howard Hamburg's and Tony Giorgio's trick."* ◆

FEEL THE
BEAT

JOHN GEORGE

AS TOLD BY JOHN GEORGE

As a full-time professional magician in the LA area, I have had the pleasure of regularly performing at events for the rich and famous. The first time I performed for a celebrity, I was a bit star-struck and my nerves got the best of me causing my knees to literally shake and my hands to tremble. I imagine this would happen to any young performer at a house party with Francis Ford Coppola and Nicolas Cage sitting in the front row.

Luckily I was quick to impress them and realized that they where reacting like any normal audience would after seeing the unbelievable. It is from this experience, and many others like it, that I was able to survive the momentous story that follows. It was like any other day in the office when I received a call from a gentleman who claimed to be the manager of an exceptionally famous person who was requesting my appearance and performance at an upcoming event. I am always skeptical about claims like this.

People use all sorts of tactics to try to convince me to lower my rates or to give them more for their dollar. However, this gentleman did not do this. He told me that he couldn't tell me who the celebrity was for security purposes. He claimed people would show up and cause a large commotion. I have to be honest. I was still thinking this guy was pulling my chain. I figured he thought his celebrity was more important or famous than he actually was. I suspected that it would be some reality-show celebrity. Nevertheless, we made an agreement and set the date and location for my performance.

The performance was to be at the world-renowned restaurant Mr. Chow in Beverly Hills. I was scheduled to perform thirty minutes of close-up magic for a small group of ten to fourteen people in a private room

HE IS BELIEVING IN MAGIC!

upstairs in the back of the restaurant. I was to meet my contact downstairs at the bar prior to going up to the room where I would perform.

Despite having doubts about who would be at this event, I had high hopes of meeting a huge star and prepared accordingly. I wore my most expensive

at Mr. Chow hoping to gain more details about whom I might be performing for. There was suspense building in my mind. The mystery was intriguing. But aside from that, I could personalize the show better if I could obtain the identity of the mystery celebrity. I sat at the bar and quickly befriended the bartender.

heard this as a well-dressed gentleman in a fitted business suit approached the bar. I think he recognized me from my web site. He introduced himself and still the anticipation grew as he refused to tell me the name of the celebrity whom I would be performing for.

HOLY CRAP, ITS ...

and best looking suit. The suit had done me well in the past. It was the suit I wore when I won the *"People's Choice Award"* at the International Brotherhood of Magician's close-up competition in New York. This suit gave me confidence. It was a striking silver Versace that demanded attention. I was ready to perform. I arrived early

He was of no help. He was used to this sort of thing and had been instructed not to tell anyone about celebrities that were dining with them. I could tell that he knew, but he wouldn't talk. So I waited and prepared for my show. The restaurant was filled with beautiful people, fancy clothes and of course, money. *"John George, is that you?"* I

The suspense began to kill me. Who could it be? He offered to buy me a drink and informed me that he would be back in ten minutes for the performance. I don't normally drink prior to a performance and don't recommend doing so. However, under these more than unusual circumstances, I ordered up a Grey Goose on the rocks with a lime. It seemed like a good idea at the moment.

The next ten minutes seemed like an eternity. For some reason being in the dark was really getting to me. Finally, I was escorted by the well dressed

That can't be. It really is him!

manager to the back of the restaurant and up the stairs. As we walked through the restaurant all of the beautiful people seemed to be staring at me. Maybe they know who is up there? Or maybe I am just imagining that they are staring at me? The suspense was at its greatest when I reached the top of the stairs and the manager's hand was resting on the doorknob waiting to open the door for me. The doorknob turned and the door was slowly opened.

I first saw a long wooden table spanning most of the room. There are coffee cups and cocktails along with the remnants of a couple of plates left from dinner on the table. There were people standing around the table speaking to one another as my gaze moved upward, I began to focus on a face. I heard the words coming from his lips and I began to register his face. *"You must be John George, our entertainment for the evening."* To my surprise and astonishment, I am now in conversation with none other than Sir Paul McCartney.

Holy Crap! Paul McCartney! Yes, Paul McCartney of the Beatles. What am I doing here? Why does Paul McCartney want to see me? What hasn't he already seen? What should I do?! This is what goes through my head as I calmly speak with Paul about where I should perform at the table. There where no shaky knees and no trembling hands on this night. I managed my excitement and kept my nerves contained.

Of course, I kept my performance as planned. I had already decided to do my best material. There was no reason to change things even though I had doubts about having the ability to entertain Sir Paul McCartney and his guests. I was floored by the response. Paul is to my left is attentive, smiling, and

> I'M GOING TO DO
> MY BEST MATERIAL

ready for magic. I performed a simple yet effective coin effect. Paul jumped to his feet and *high-fives* me. This is a huge moment for me. Not just for that day, but forever. It was a defining moment in my life as a performer. In that moment I understood that Sir Paul McCartney is Paul. He is just Paul and I am entertaining him along with all of his guests. He isn't a Beatle. He isn't a superstar. In that moment, in that

ON THE BUSINESS, WE CALL THIS "A" MATERIAL

room, he is Paul and I am the superstar performing for him. His guests are watching me, not him. He is watching me. He is believing the magic. They are believing it too. They have bought into my performance and are in the moment. I am in the moment, and I feel I am in my element doing what I do best. I am not fazed by anything. I felt unstoppable and know they will like what I have planned next. This allowed me to be myself and continue with confidence. It is what I have been studying and perfecting for years. I know they will

scream and be surprised. I finish the show to applause, smiles, and sounds of amazement from everyone in the audience. I was having fun.

Unbelievably the story doesn't end here. I had performed for forty-five minutes, which had exceeded what I had agreed to do by fifteen minutes. I had done all of my best material, everything that consistently got the best reactions. In the business we call this our "A" material. As a perfectionist, I claim to only have "A" material. If it isn't "A" material, I stop doing it. As

a result, my repertoire isn't as big as many other magicians that have "B" and "C" material. This has never been a problem in the past, and I didn't suspect this night would be any different. And so the story continues.

At the conclusion of my scheduled performance, Paul asked me what I am going to do now that I was done. I had no plans. I told Paul that I would probably go home and have dinner with my wife, watch some television, and go to sleep. I actually said that! In hindsight, I wished I would have made something

Sure I had done other things in the past

up to sound a bit more hip and cool. Paul asked if I would do another *"set."* Nobody has ever asked me to do another *"set."* I have been asked to stay longer, to perform more, to stay and do some more magic. But never have I been asked to do another *"set."* It was pretty cool to be asked to do another *"set"*, and how could I turn down Paul? I told Paul I would love to perform another set. He suggested I go downstairs and take *"fifteen."* It is at this point in the story that I am particularly proud of myself as a businessman. I take pride in being a good businessman. I walked over to the well dressed man in the corner, Paul's manager. I can't believe I did this, but I leaned in and quietly said, *"You realize this is going to cost more than we agreed upon?"* We exited the room and I renegotiated with Paul's manager. The next fifteen minutes were

the longest fifteen minutes of my life. I had just performed all of my magic and I had to come up with a second set. I had no more. At the time that was all I had in my regular working repertoire.

Sure I had done other things in the past. I had other tricks that I used to do. But remember these were not *"A"* material tricks. I had thrown them out

they didn't love my magic, but rather they loved me. I hoped this anyway? I hoped they asked me back because they liked me and enjoyed my presence. I stopped worrying about what I would do and I consciously decided that they would love what ever I did because they liked me as a performer. They had bought into me and my story and

WANNA DO ANOTHER SET?

for a reason. So I sat at the bar thinking and making notes and trying to decide how to entertain *"Sir Paul McCartney."* Somehow, Paul once again became *"Sir Paul McCartney"* when I left the room. I went back and forth about what to do. I struggled until I realized something. For some reason I got it in my mind that

they were going to follow me down whatever road I lead them. I had no idea what I did for them. I can't remember a single thing I did during that second set. But I do remember it was fun. It was fun for me and it was fun for them. It was a nice place to be. And once again this would be a good story if it ended here.

COULDN'T KEEP THE BEAT!

It does not. I am on cloud nine, and I thought, *"It can't get any better."* I just performed a second set for Paul and his friends. They reacted just as positively as they had on my first set. What could make this any better?

As I picked up my props and prepared to leave Paul asked me to sit and talk to him. I sat down and Paul asked me a couple of things about myself and how I learned what I do. I answered. Then I was struck by what followed. Paul turned and asked me, *"Is there anything I can do for you?"* This really caught me off guard. What does he mean? What can he do for me? He asked if I

had any questions or if there is anything I wanted to know. I'm sitting with Sir. Paul McCartney, and I now feel like I am just sitting with a friend that I have known for years. He was easy to talk to and was interested in me and my life.

He also knew that I was interested in him. I wish I could have prepared for this. The first thing I asked was to get a picture with him. As previously mentioned, I came prepared knowing there might be a celebrity at the event.

I had brought my digital camera and Paul was happy to oblige. His manager took many pictures and Paul posed with enthusiasm as did his friends.

I then told Paul I was learning to play the drums and I asked if he had any advice for me. He said, *"Yes, keep the beat"* with a big smile and a laugh. We spoke some more and talked about many things. I then asked why the Beatles got rid of their original drummer Pete Best. Paul grinned again and then exclaimed, *"He couldn't keep the beat!!! He couldn't keep the beat!"* I joined his laughter. We talked some more and I spoke with the other people at the party. I was welcome to stay.

I eventually left. I walked outside and there was paparazzi and groves of people waiting to get an autograph or just a glimpse of Sir Paul McCartney.

I drove home and had dinner with my wife. Needless to say, we did not watch television that night.

I told her this story. ♦

THE ELEPHANT WAS ESCORTED OUT
— A Big Surprise *page 245*

So I started thinking quickly and I stood up. I was about three feet behind Larry. Remember his back was to me. I watched Larry carefully because I knew a certain move was coming.
— I Hate Card Tricks *page 215*

POSSIBLY HOUDINI'S MOST FAMOUS FEAT
— Icy Escape *page 213*

Since 2005, I've successfully pulled over 400 cons and scams for the BBC TV Show ...
— The Cheat *page 217*

But
he did
catch
a cold.

ICY ESCAPE

HARRY HOUDINI

As Told by Ivan Amodei

Harry Houdini was a fantastic marketer. That is why he is one of the top ten most recognizable names in the world. Houdini was, in fact, very competitive when it came to his career. By 1905, Europe had been saturated with Houdini, the self-proclaimed *"Handcuff King."* His American audience demanded he return to the states and begin performing there.

He packed the theaters. For the majority of his career, Houdini performed his act as a headliner in vaudeville. He was the highest-paid performer in American theater. In today's dollars, Houdini was earning about $100,000 per month. And for several years, Houdini's stunts (*with advertising and marketing*) kept him a constant household name.

Possibly Houdini's most famous stunt was his jump from the Belle Isle Bridge into the icy Detroit River. As the story accounts, on November 27, 1906, Harry Houdini, after being locked into two sets of handcuffs, jumped off the bridge and into a hole that had been cut in the ice. He did not resurface. Panic spread throughout the crowd. Houdini's assistants knew that he couldn't hold his breath for more than three and a half minutes.

After about three minutes, they realized that the current had carried him downstream. The emergency plan was to have a roped man dive in after him. No one was eager to do this, so a rope was thrown into the hole. His wife, who had stayed at a nearby hotel, was quickly informed, *"Houdini drowned! Houdini drowned!"*

Meanwhile, having freed himself, Houdini found that he could breath from air pockets that were trapped between the water and the ice. Hours passed when he finally saw the rope, he grabbed it and climbed out of the hole. Cheers rang out from the crowd, and he was

> # COME SEE THE GREAT HOUDINI!

met by his wife, who was in tears. Well, that all NEVER HAPPENED! Houdini created that entire story. Because so few reporters actually showed up for the jump into the icy river, Houdini thought he was not going to get any publicity at all.

So he got on his typewriter and wrote an article about how Houdini (*writing as a reporter that witnessed it*) barely escaped from the icy depths of a freezing river and almost died.

A little known fact was of the many newspaper articles that were written about Houdini were actually written by him under another name he used. N. Osey was a name that he created and used to write vaudeville gossip columns in England.

If you take a closer look at the name and group them together without the period you get the word — NOSEY. He

Did You Know?

Erich Weiss (HOUDINI)
March 24, 1874 — October 31, 1926

Houdini was a movie producer and actor, a magician, an escape artist and an exposer of fraudulent mediums. He was also one of the first people to pilot an airplane in Australia.

would often write comments about other shows and often degrade and discredit his competitors. On the other hand, he would promote his own show and write complimentary statements in the paper such as, *"Everyone must not miss the show of THE GREAT HOUDINI!"* Its

an inspirational story of how to take anything negative and turn it into a positive. Its a tale that actually stuck with his career and became a part of his legend and unbelievable magic history.

Amazing! ♦

I HATE CARD TRICKS

LARRY JENNINGS

AS TOLD BY HOWARD HAMBURG

We are all sitting in the Vernon corner of the World Famous Magic Castle. We were directly outside the close-up room. All the legends were there that night, Charlie Miller, Mike Skinner, Larry Jennings, Dai Vernon and myself just all there talking.

There was a large line to the close-up room that extended out through the bar. So the line wrapped around and came close to us. There were about five women standing in line talking to the Professor Dai Vernon.

The Professor looked up at me and said, *"Howard, would you do something for my friends, please would you do something for them?"* I got up and offered one of them to select a card (Ten of Hearts) and then had another person selected a card too (Three of Clubs).

THAT WAS TERRIBLE!

The cards were returned to the deck and shuffled. I asked the first person what their card was? With an empty hand, I went into my pocket and removed the first card. I then approached the second person that selected a card, and with my hand cupped around the first person's card I said, *"And what was your card?"* She replied, *"The three of clubs."* I said, *"Don't take your eyes off the deck."* I immediately uncupped my hands and there was just the Three of Clubs. The entire deck had VANISHED! Its a wonderful effect and always gets a great response. The ladies thank me and I sat back down. The Professor thanked me too. Larry Jennings, who has had a

couple (*if you know what I mean*) looked at me and said, *"That was the worst F**ing thing I have ever seen! Should*

LARRY IS REALLY GOING TO BE PISSED OFF!

have done a top cover pass. Geez, why the hell do you do it that way. That was terrible!" Dai then replied, *"Larry, you know Howard is a friend of ours."* Then Charlie comments, *"Larry, if you have something to say about what someone does, maybe you can say it in a more constructive way by showing them."* Larry got up and said, *"I'll show um."*

Larry approached the same group of ladies I just did the card trick to. He proceeded to do the **exact card trick** for them. The exact one. His back was

to me. In the meantime, the Professor said to me, *"Howard, that's terrible what he did to you, just terrible, that's really bad."* Charlie agreed. The Professor continued, *"I noticed Larry is using Ryder Back Reds and you have the same deck. Maybe you can think of something?"* Vernon was thinking ahead. I started thinking quickly and the solution came to me. I stood up. I was about three-feet behind Larry. I watched him very carefully. You see, I knew a certain move was coming.

Secretly, you need to ditch the deck into your left coat pocket at a certain time in the trick. Of course,

without anyone knowing that is what is happening. I simply waited behind Larry until he went for the pocket to dispose the deck. As he did, I threw my deck between his legs. They splattered all over the floor in front of him and in front of these five women. He immediately thought that he had missed his pocket and that the entire deck fell to the floor and he screwed up this trick badly.

He saw all the cards all over the floor and became furious. He rumbled up the stairs mumbling, *"Really bad word, this is Sh#@!$. Bunch of very, very bad words. Jerks, Jerks, As@#$%^!!!"*

I got back to the couch and Vernon was sitting there with that twinkle in his eye. The Professor said, *"Larry is really going to pissed off later when he finds his deck in his pocket."* ◆

THE
CHEAT

R. PAUL WILSON

As Told By R. Paul Wilson

Making mistakes as a performer has repercussions. You might lose the audience, your confidence or even a client. When cheating someone, there's a chance you might lose your *life, your liberty or your testicles*. Any way you look

---

YOU MIGHT LOSE YOUR TESTICLES!

---

at it, the dangers of cheating are much greater than those of performing. Of course, I am not a cheat. After a lifetime of study and research into the subject, I do consider myself to be an expert, and in recent years, I've been given the opportunity to build a

wealth of experience. Since 2005, I've successfully pulled over four-hundred cons and scams for the BBC TV Show *The Real Hustle*. Before that, myself and *"my team"* demonstrated a dozen ways to beat casinos and security systems on the Court TV show *Takedown*, and, in the late 90s, I spent a few years working with professional Blackjack and Roulette teams before it occurred to me that his might not be the best career for a father of two. As I've said, I'm not a cheat, but I have cheated for real, and to be frank, I'm not proud of it. Thankfully,

the Gods were against me, and I learned an expensive but valuable lesson. In my opinion, mistakes are the paving stones towards success. Cheating is like that. Sure, there's a larger margin for error, but I've come close a few times in the real world. Looking back, I can't believe the situations I put myself in.

For example, holding out (*retaining cards in your hand*) in live casino games. Dealing deuces (*dealing the second card from the top of the deck*) for hardened gamblers. And even loading a high-stakes private game with marked decks. None of this made me any money. Not one cent.

For the most part, I was just messing around, testing my chops, trying to learn. As a result, I turned into a decent, though not brilliant, poker player. I won

Magic's Most Amazing Stories **217**

THE RATCATCHER AND CHICKEN GEORGE

a few tournaments and eventually got invited to private games and played for higher stakes. I attended these games several times, playing on the square (*not cheating*), but one night, I gave into temptation and learned a lesson I'll never forget. It's the last time I deliberately tried to beat/cheat someone for real money.

I won't say my competitor's name, but he was widely despised by most of the players in Glasgow. He was an odious man who treated everyone with open contempt and had all the charm of a rattlesnake. Worst of all, he was a damn good player. He and I were the last two players in a hefty hand of seven card stud. I had the deal and was, as usual, playing on the square.

That night, I had enjoyed some success with a few well chosen plays, and a healthy helping of chips. On one particular hand, he decided to go all in. He had some hearts up, and I was worried about him having a flush (*all the same suit*). I had two pair: **Aces and Kings**. His last card was another heart, so chances were good that he had two in the hole (*face down cards*). If I was correct, I needed an Ace or King to beat his hand with a full house. About six other players were watching very closely. I couldn't call his hand. The odds were against me.

When he pushed all his chips in, I felt all the pressure of the moment bearing down on me. I knew I had to fold, but somehow, I found myself asking how much was in the pot? As I gestured towards the huge pile of chips, I peeked the top card of my deck and spotted a King, just the card I NEEDED. It was an unforgivable thing to do in an honest game, but no one even felt the move. Suddenly, I was in a position to win if I had the balls to move with all that heat on me.

I thought about it for a long time then, I *"CALLED"* his hand. Without it, my opponent's flush had me beat. I was being watched by every player at the table, and NOW I needed to deal a *"second"* to keep the TOP CARD — the King for myself.

I heard myself say, *"Good luck."* My opponent sneered. Everyone laughed, and I dealt the best *"deuce"* of my life. The second card floated across the table and landed in front of him. Then I fairly dealt the King to myself. I had made my

full house. You may not believe this, but I immediately felt bad. Apart from the adrenaline, which causes the gut to tighten, I genuinely felt guilty. These were people I liked and admired. They had invited me into their game, and I had just done the unspeakable. There's nothing I hate more than a thief and here I was, stealing from the table.

"*He's a mug, I got him beat,*" my opponent boasted. Someone defended me, but he was adamant. "*He should have folded. I had you beat with a flush,*" he stated. Sure enough, five of his cards were hearts. My guilt was soon washed away by my desire to put him in his place, so I turned my *down-cards* UP to show the full house. My opponent was angry. Some of the players laughed, and I let out a silent sigh of relief, but the moment was short lived. One of the other players noticed something everyone, including my opponent missed. His hand was not just a flush — it was a **straight flush**: five hearts, in order, from four to eight! He had actually beat my full house. I stared

> HE'S A MUG, I GOT HIM BEAT.

at his hand, as another player helpfully put the cards in order. It was unbearable as I watched every penny I had get pulled into his stack.

As I left the house, I almost threw up. Not because of the money. I never played with money I couldn't lose, but because of what I had attempted. As the fresh air hit me, I suddenly realized what I had risked to win a hand of cards.

Had that "*second deal*" caught a hanger (*missed the deal completely*), I would definitely have woken up in the hospital, or floating down the River Clyde. As I caught my breath, something else struck me. The fifth heart that made him his straight flush was the last card I had dealt him — the "*second deal.*" Had I just dealt *fairly* off the top and given him the King that was there, I would have beaten his hand with my two solid pairs!

For months afterward, people would mention that hand as a jibe to my opponent. He had a straight flush and didn't even know it! Every time they did, I felt that tightening at the pit of my stomach. I never cheated in a real game again. The way I saw it was *Lady Luck* wasn't going to stand for it and I could live without the bad karma. ♦

Heeere's TC

As Told by TC Tahoe

May 1990, I found myself driving up the scenic Pacific Coast Highway, heading towards Monterey California.

I was booked to perform at a club called *The Boiler Room*. It featured bands and comedians on the weekend.

I had been working very hard in LA. and was looking forward to this "*get-a-way*." Little did I know that the manager of the *Boiler Room*, Lesley, would turn out to be a charming redhead from Scotland that would steal my heart and just three short months later would become my wife. It was only because I fell for Lesley that I agreed to do a free benefit show on that Sunday afternoon.

A local girl had gone missing a few weeks before, the police had called off the search, so family and friends were holding a benefit to raise money to continue the search privately. I have to admit that this is not a gig I would have agreed to do under normal circumstances. Normal circumstances being not falling in love and agreeing to anything to impress a wee Scottish lass!

HOW FUNNY SHOULD I BE?

YIKES!

Two bands played that Sunday afternoon. A lot of people turned out, a local restaurant catered and I was scheduled to go on and do my show. I was under no illusions, even with the bands, the food and all the people, this was going to be a solemn occasion. I was desperately trying to figure out *"how funny"* to be. Before I knew it, the time for my performance had crept up on me. A man I didn't know got up and said a few words. *"Not good,"* I remember thinking. The Band had just finished, it would have been best to bring me right on.

This man turned out to be a friend of the missing girl. Here are the few words he said.

"I want to thank everyone for coming out this afternoon. As you know we were here to raise money to continue the search for Melissa, unfortunately they found Melissa's body this morning, so the money raised will go for her funeral."

A long silence followed, broken by a few people softly crying. Then he continued, *"I believe we have a comedy magician now."* He pointed at me and walked away from the microphone. Never have the words *"The Show Must Go On"* rung louder in my ears.

On the upside, I am still happily married to Lesley. ♦

Did You Know?

The famous magician Dr. Walford Bodie was not as funny as everyone thought. He cheated a little. He secretly used laughing gas on his volunteers to induce laughter.

Since laughter is contagious, this made his audience also burst into hysterics.

MAGIC FINGER

DAVID MINKIN

AS TOLD BY DAVID MINKIN

Yolanda and Josephine come each week to clean my house and keep my mess in check. In broken English, they speak with me, and I respond in broken Spanish.

We all have a good time with it. For years, these two sweet little ladies have cleaned my house without incident. One day, I was sitting at my desk when I heard whispers coming from around the corner. I tried to make out what they were saying, but couldn't.

A moment later, the whispers turned into *blood-curdling* screams, and both ladies began yelling frantically in Spanish. I came around the corner and saw them looking down at the floor at what appeared to be a dismembered finger. Yolanda shouted, *"Why you make it follow me?!"* I said, *"What do*

IT FOLLOW YOLANDA!

you mean?" Josephine responded, *"The finger … it follow Yolanda!"* Yolanda tried to make a break for it and get away from the magic finger. She jumped over it, and looked back, but the finger began to move toward her.

It was following her! She screamed in horror and ran off again. I began to laugh uncontrollably as I realized it was only a fake rubber finger, but to them, it was a real finger. I could understand, it looked just like a real finger. One of the girls had accidentally knocked it onto the floor while cleaning. The really

funny part was attached to the finger was some INVISIBLE THREAD of mine. It was for a trick that I did. The thread had somehow attached itself to her shoe.

I'll never forget the image of that tiny woman running at full speed down my hallway, screaming in Spanish, as that finger chased after her.

To this day, Yolanda refuses to believe that I didn't purposely cause the finger to chase her. And the three of us still laugh about it. ♦

chapter
nine

Being naive, bad timing, screaming women, plants, The Magic Castle, ducks, Houdini trains, famous people, bullets and more

MR. DICK

SIMON LOVELL

AS TOLD BY SIMON LOVELL

You know those moments where you wish that instead of doing what you did, you'd just dropped dead instead? Well this was one of those moments for me.

I was a very young man, at one of my very first magic conventions and very excited to be there. Imagine my thrill when, across the room, I noticed a group of three magicians chatting.

I'd seen two of them on television! Wow, some really famous guys! With a complete lack of respect that can only come from extreme youth, I bustled up to them and thrust out my autograph book. With much better manners than I had displayed, the first magician very politely signed my book.

I got the book and thrust it into the hands of the second famous magician who also graciously signed it. I stammered a *"thank you,"* and turned to leave. *"Don't you want Dick's signature too?"* replied one of the famous guys.

"Are you famous too Mr. Dick?" I asked, turning back toward him.

He took my book and signed. He said, *"You never know, I may be some day."* The other two seemed to find this rather funny and amusing.

I didn't look at the last signature until a few days later. When I did, I nearly dropped dead with shame. The only words I'd said were, *"Are you famous too Mr. Dick?"* I never met him again and can only hope that there is an afterlife, so that I can apologize to him.

Oh the magician? It was the most famous Richard Cardini! ♦

ARE YOU THE FAMOUS MR. DICK?

WHICH WAY?

STEVE BEAM

AS TOLD BY SIMON LOVELL

Perhaps Steve Beam is best known as the publisher of the now, sadly defunct, *Trapdoor Magazine*, as well as, the author of his excellent volumes: SEMI-AUTOMATIC CARD TRICKS. He is a very witty and funny guy and a joy to be around. I've only seen him at a total loss for words once.

It all happened on the way to a lecture. In the car was Steve, his friend Wayne, and myself. Steve was in CT on a lecture tour, and I offered to guide him to the lecture, as well as, put the mad duo up for the night.

We entered North Haven and found the lecture hall easily. It was all going far too easily, but then Steve announced that he was hungry. Even though he's a skinny guy (*he makes me look fat*) he takes food pretty seriously! We drove up the road, spotted a diner and entered. What could go wrong?

After the meal, we started to drive back to the hall. Steve made a right turn and I noticed that we were a block short. *"No problem at all,"* he said, with his deep southern accent, *"We'll just take the next left."* Steve made the next left — straight onto the Amtrack line that runs through the town. Worse still, the rails were high and the car was jammed onto them. He tried reversing to no avail. *"What do you think we should do?"* he said, oblivious to the danger, *"Get out of the car NOW! Do you know what a train could do to this car?"* We leapt out and it seemed like only minutes later that there were police cars everywhere, including a special railway police guy.

Two trains were held up while we waited for a tow truck. Even a local TV news station turned up to film the event. We declined to be interviewed as none of us wanted to look like the village idiot!

Steve finally did the lecture after getting an inch thick pile of tickets, but at least, on the way home, we eventually saw the funny side of it all.

Steve started referring to himself as, *"A trained magician who was railroaded into making the wrong turn!"* ◆

> ## WRONG TURN!

My timing was so thrown off, that moves I can easily do in my sleep became completely awkward and unnatural.

— THE AUDITION *page 57*

GREAT INTRO

CURTIS KAM

AS TOLD BY CURTIS KAM

I have had a number of beautiful girls as assistants and only one of them was, well let's say, *"easily distracted."* In one show, we were set to go on right after a comedian. This girl wanted to watch the guy's act. She asked if it was okay to go out into the audience and watch it from there?

Against my better judgment, I said she could, but needed to be on-stage immediately after because we were the next act. The emcee great and after the comedian was finished, he began our long intro. I wrote a long intro on purpose so everyone working with me could get into proper position in plenty of time. Not this time! The music started. I ran out on-stage from stage right and immediately produced a guy *assistant* in a puff of smoke. Its an amazing illusion. Then I gestured to stage left for the girl to come out and do our next fantastic illusion. But she's not there. No assistant anywhere to be found. I looked backstage, to my left and to my right. Nothing, no girl. Where the hell is she?

No THIS TIME

I told her to be ready. It felt like a lifetime up there, but in reality it was probably 30 seconds and still no girl. Then finally out of the corner of my eye, I saw someone running really fast through the audience toward the stage. It was her. But she was supposed to be on-stage for the illusion. Later on, after my set, I went up to her and asked what had happened? She said that she was sitting in the audience watching the comedian and then started to hear the intro to us. She completely forgot that she was part of the next act and got really rapped up in the intro.

She started telling the people next to her that this next act sounds really great and said, *"WOW, this next act sounds really, really great. I can't wait to see this."*

Then it hit her when she saw me looking around wondering where she was and then she realized that SHE was part of that act.

Here is my dilemma: *do I shorten the intros, drop all my assistants and just stick to doing card tricks?* ◆

S WAIT A SECOND

MARTIN NASH

AS TOLD BY IVAN AMODEI

About 1997, I was at The Magic Castle when I spotted Martin Nash sitting at the bar in front of the Close-Up Room.

Let me preface by stating that Martin passed away in 2009 and was considered to be one of the top card men in the world. He could do things with cards few people could and was one of the nicest people you would ever want to know or meet. I had never met him, but had to go over and introduce myself. I said, *"Hi Martin, I'm Ivan Amodei and it's a pleasure to meet you. Would it be too much to ask you to demonstrate your second deal to me so I can see it really up close."* He showed me. Let me tell you, it looked like he dealt the top card. But it was the second card. But how? I said, *"WOW, that is amazing."* He replied, *"Would you like me to show you the work on it?"* I was floored. He offered to show me the technique and we just met. That was the kind of guy he was. Very kind. After he showed me, I decide to master it no matter how long it took. Let's fast forward about seven to eight years now. I am working a week performing in the Close-up room at The Magic Castle. Martin was there and walked right up to me, but he didn't remember me from our meeting many years earlier. He said, *"So I hear I should*

DO THAT AGAIN! DO THAT AGAIN. ONE MORE TIME.

That was the best I have ever seen

see this show." I said, *"Would you like to be my guest?"* He replied, *"Thank you so much!"* I replied, *"Martin, don't you remember many years ago you were so kind enough to show me your second deal and also tip all the work on it."* He said, *"WOW, great, how does it look?"* I replied, *"Great, I'll show you after the show."* I finished my show and he came up to talk to me. After a few minutes, he said, *"So let's see that second deal I taught you."* I removed a deck of cards and spread them face down on the table. I had him remove only one card.

I very slowly placed the selected card below the top card so that he knew there was no suspicious stuff happening. I then did the deal for him. He stared at me and said, *"Do it again!"* So I did. He replied, *"Do it again!"* So I it again and again and again. I did it at least seven times in a row for him.

He told me it was the best second deal he had ever seen. Better than his, and better than anything on earth he's ever seen. Now you're asking, am I blowing my own horn? NO! NO! NO!

I played a practical joke on Martin. I knew that he was going to ask me to show him this deal after my show. We talked about it before hand. I purposely told him that I would rather wait to show him until after my show and not before. You see Martin never looked at the entire deck. He took my word for it that all the cards were normal like a regular deck should be. In fact, the entire deck was the ***five of hearts***. But since he never thought to look through them, I never thought to tell him. I know exactly what he was thinking. *"Man, that looks exactly like it is coming off the top!"* IT WAS! I could have demonstrated bottom deals and even center deals, but I thought to stop while I was ahead.

I had one of the best card men in the world believing that he taught me his second deal and then I went and mastered it better than him.

Now, we all know the truth. ◆

I'M BACK

ED ALONZO
AS TOLD BY ED ALONZO

A few years ago, I was appearing at the La Mirada Civic theater in Orange County California. I ended my show that night with an effect called *"Crazy Duck Cargo Net."* Like a regular CARGO NET illusion, but different. Briefly, a white Peking duck drives a small car around the stage while being chased by a lovely female dancer dressed as a sexy police officer.

The officer dances to the music and directs the driving duck into an open front box which is then raised into the air via some cables. An empty glass framed box is brought out on-stage, a dancer shows it to be empty, and then covers it with a cloth. She then grabs a long cable that is hanging from the

CRAZY DUCK CARGO NET

suspended box, pulls on it, the box explodes and falls apart hanging in pieces. The car and duck have vanished. Now the police girl with her back to the audience pulls off the cloth from the glass box on-stage and we see the duck and car have appeared inside.

The dancer covers herself with the cloth for a moment and drops it. She has magically changed into me.

During this performance something different happened. I had done the magical transposition with the female dancer correctly, but as my back was to the audience (*I'm secretly dressed as the girl dancer*), I backed up a bit too close to the edge of the stage after revealing the duck and car reappeared.

I pulled the cloth up to cover my face. As I turned around to show that the dancer has changed into me (*I was now standing at the very edge of the*

orchestra pit and I didn't realized I was that close), and take my BIG BOW, I fell off the stage (*eight feet*) and into the pit. I landed on a drum set. First I hit the cymbal, then the snare drum, and everything else down there. Moments later, I crawled out of the pit, back onto the stage and again took another bow. It was as if the girl changed into me, then I suddenly disappeared. An illusion I'd rather not repeat ever again. I was lucky the band was off that night. ♦

MAGIC BOOKS

Books on magic began to appear late in the 16th century.

One of the earliest was published in France in 1584, *The First Part of Subtle and Pleasant Tricks* by Jean Prevost.

READY, AIM
FIRE

CHUNG LING SOO

As Told by Ivan Amodei

The controversy surrounding William Ellsworth Robinson still lingers today nearly 100 years after his unexpected death. He was well-known in the United States at the time, as *"The Man of Mystery."*

In an attempt to reinvent himself, William took the name Chung Ling Soo, a variation of a well-known Chinese magician named Ching Ling Foo and also performed many of the same effects Ching made famous.

With appropriate Chinese costume, makeup and paraphernalia, William established a *new* act, and began performing throughout Europe as his new creation Chung Ling Soo.

It was 1905, London, Soo setup shop in a theatre across from his rival, Ching. Both men claimed to be the *"Original Chinese Conjurers."* This developed into a spiteful relationship with one another. Public debate over who was the best swept through the streets. Though

actually American, Soo maintained the illusion of being a Chinese master of the magical arts.

He lived and breathed his character and persona from the stage, even to the extent that he never spoke English in public, especially to journalists. He always was accompanied by a translator to complete the deceit.

Chung and Ching continued their feud and often challenged one another to a *"show-down of skills"* to prove

HIS NEW CREATION, CHUNG LING SOO

who was indeed the better magician. On one night, they both agreed to perform a series of effects in front of a live audience and let the people crown *"the best magician."* To everyone's surprise, Ching never appeared to the dual. It was on the dark night of March 23rd 1918, in the *Edwardian-Style*, Wood Green Empire Theatre in North London, that Chung performed CONDEMNED TO DEATH BY THE BOXERS for the last time. In today's words, this effect is simply called, THE BULLET CATCH. Two guns were brought to the stage by assistants dressed in boxer costumes. Bullet's were also presented. One gun is decided on, as well as, a bullet by an audience member. This spectator marks the bullet with red ink, identifying it as his/her personal mark. Members of the audience also examine the copper-coloured slug verifying that it is the only one of its kind. Tensions mount as everyone realizes what will happen next.

Quiet chitchat turned to whispers, and whispers turn to silence, as the gun was loaded with this lone, identifiable round. Quickly, silence swept over the beautiful ornate theatre. The hefty firearm is loaded with this single ink-scarred bullet. An assistant aims the

COMPLETELY UNLIKE
OTHER PERFORMANCES

weapon directly at Chung's chest. The gun is fired. Smoke filled the silent stage. Hundreds of times prior to this day, the bullet was easily caught by the skillful Chung with his bare-hand.

Almost as if magically, snatching the ammo out of mid-air. Sometimes even catching it between his teeth. Then, as might be expected, ending the illusion by showing the signed slug to the original owner and audience members.

But this time, *whether by design or destiny*, it went devastatingly wrong. Chung's hand swept across the path of the bullet, in an attempt to catch it, but suddenly Chung fell to the floor — completely unlike other performances of this piece. His stage assistants and crew quickly rushed to his side. Unbeknownst to Chung and everyone gathered around him, the bullet had pierced his chest. Chung had been shot

in front of a live audience. And for the first time, since creating the character Chung Ling Soo, and as he laid their bleeding, he spoke English, and uttered, *"Oh my God. Something's happened. Lower the curtain."* The illusion of being both Chinese and a Master Magician ended at that exact moment.

William Ellsworth Robinson, *aka* Chung Ling Soo (1861–1918) died the next day in a hospital not far from the beautiful theatre he was shot in.

In a lengthy court case that followed, the judge declared it *"accidental death"* after Chung's wife revealed the secrets and details of the trick. This however, did not cease rumours and suspicions surrounding his death.

Buzz circled that it could it have been suicide because his wife was having an elicit affair with his agent. Others implied that it was murder and on that

historic night, the spectator that handled the gun was a secret accomplice planted by a rival magician to manipulate the weapon so that Chung would be killed.

Although no proof supports any of these theories, Chung Ling Soo's death is still synonymous with one of magic's most extraordinary theatrical tragedies.♦

Story references:
Randi, James. Conjuring.
(St. Martin's Press, 1992)
ISBN 0-312-09771-9 page 78

Randi, James. Conjuring.
(St. Martin's Press, 1992)
ISBN 0-312-09771-9 page 81

Randi, James. Conjuring.
(St. Martin's Press, 1992)
ISBN 0-312-09771-9 page 84

Jim Steinmeyer – Newsletter – Spring 2005
— Glorious Deception

HE WAS BOOKED FOR A SIX WEEK RUN IN A SMALL THEATRE IN ENGLAND. HE HAD TO DO EIGHT SHOWS A WEEK AND EACH SHOW USED UP *three condoms.*

— BETTER SAFE THAN SORRY *page 249*

I think he was packing heat

— A NIGHT TO FORGET *page 124*

OH NO, ITS GONE

CARL ANDREWS

AS TOLD BY CARL ANDREWS

When you do magic and you decide to perform effects with a spectator's ring, you had better make sure you don't do anything too crazy. I can guarantee you their eyes will be peeled to you, so you will definitely have their attention during your performance. Here is what happened to me.

I was table hopping at an outdoor cafe one night. While performing ring flight (*this effect is where a ring is borrowed and vanished. Then the ring is discovered linked onto a key link on a set of keys that I have in my pocket*) and I begin the routine. I asked to borrow a young lady's ring. I proceed to vanish it. I have done this hundreds of times. Disaster just struck. The reel inside the key chain retracted with the ring on it and instead of quietly going into my pocket, I heard the sound of metal hitting the ground. *"Oh no,"* I thought! I knew what had happened, but could tell I was the only one. It had fallen on the ground somewhere. I quickly looked on the floor and around the area and could not see it anywhere. I just lost the ring she generously handed me. How do I get out of this?

I whispered to a passing busboy what had happened. He casually started to look for the ring. While he was looking for the ring, I stalled the audience at the table. I began doing more magic for the them as if this was what I had planned all along. After a few more effects, I started walking away. The lady who's

HEY, WHERE IS MY RING?

ring I borrowed yelled out, *"Hey Carl, where is my ring?"* No one knew this, but lucky for me the bus boy found the ring unharmed and secretly returned it to me. I didn't want to immediately produce it after he gave it to me, so I decided to continue the illusion and that this was part of the whole plan.

I knew they were going to say something to me and not let me walk away without giving back the ring.

To my surprise, it was her engagement ring. She just got engaged a week earlier and the ring was worth a LOT of money. I can't say how much, but here's a hint. I would need a bank loan to replace it. ◆

THE PLANT

DANIEL SYLVESTER "SYLVESTER THE JESTER"

AS TOLD BY DANIEL SYLVESTER

Looking back I should have flown home. Instead, I decided to call my aunt that lived rear San Francisco where I had just done a show. She told me that her son, my cousin, was visiting and that he was able to drive me back home to Orange County! Wow, a road trip with Brian! I'm there!

I visited with the relatives for a day and then Brian and I set off on our road trip to LA. His car, however, was a miniature French job called a *Le Car,* and it could hardly contain the two of us, let alone all my magic gear. Nevertheless, we took to the road with great enthusiasm.

It was great fun for awhile. Beautiful landscapes whizzed by while Bob Dylan and the Rolling Stones supplied the sound track. But then as the sunset faded, Brian's car started making whirling noises. We were about 20 miles from where Brian lived, in San Luis Obispo, when we sputtered to a stop in the dark on a mountain road. Luckily, I had tools!

Well, sort of. I had my fake jumper cables, my sledgehammer and an anvil, too. All my magic props. These might have been useful had we been on a horse and buggy. You should know this was a time before cell phones. Anyway, we figured that we'd have to spend the night there on the side of the road and hoped someone might stop to give us a lift into town. Being 6´2˝, Brian decided to sleep outside on the ground. I, on the other hand at a mere 5´7˝, figured sleeping in the car had to be better then the cold ground. When morning came

IT WAS UNBEARABLE!

around, I wriggled, with great effort, out of the vehicle like a mangled circus freak squeezing out of a tiny, clown car. I was just in time to hear the air brakes of a trucker stopping to give us a lift.

He only had room for one so I to stayed behind. I hadn't slept much so I didn't object and besides, the sun was coming up on the hillside and it looked like a warm and inviting place to catch up on lost sleep. I flopped like a dead fish to the hillside's soft foliage. Five hours later, I was awaken by the sound of a tow truck. For that moment it seemed like everything might just work out. Sure our trip to LA was scrapped.

Laid in the plant life from head to toe

HOW ABOUT SOME YELLOWS?

My cousin explained, *"You could simply take the Trailways bus from San Luis Obispo all the way back to Orange County."* It didn't turn out to be as easy as he suspected, especially without the car. By the time we actually got to the station, there was only one bus left so I ran to buy the ticket and ran again to catch the bus. All while carrying my heavy magic gear. Finally on the bus and out of breath, I put my head against the seat back and tried to settle in.

I soon found that I was sitting next to a grinning, shaggy looking *Dead Head* who was overly friendly me and said, *"You want some hash man? No? Well, how about some yellows? It'll help you sleep. No? I got some coke, too. You want a little?"* He said. He seemed befuddled by my reluctance. Maybe it had something to do with the big purple hat I was wearing. Finally he offered me some brownies! *"Do they have walnuts in 'em?"* I asked, practically drooling. *"No, but they've got pot in 'em,"* he replied. *"Thanks anyway,"* I sighed.

Suddenly, I began to wonder why we weren't leaving and where had our bus driver gone? He'd been gone for over 15-minutes and that soon turned into 25-minutes. Finally, a woman from Trailways came aboard to explain to us that our bus driver had picked this day and this hour to quit his job! The worse part was that she said a the new driver wouldn't get there for another hour.

That meant I might likely be too late to catch a connecting bus in Los Angeles. She gave us all bus vouchers and said good luck. Oh God! I groaned, I should have taken all that guy's drugs when I had the chance.

I was quite exhausted and slept most of the way. In fact, I have no memory of the journey which made me think maybe the *Dead Head* slipped me something. The next thing I knew it was dark and we were pulling into Los Angeles. In the mayhem, I grabbed my gear and dashed to catch the last bus to Orange County.

But then a policeman yelled, *"Hey you! Whadda ya think yur' doin'?"* *"Catchin' that bus,"* I said. *"Maybe."* He replied, *"But first you're gonna get this ticket for jaywalking."* *"Ah, come on man! That's the last bus! I gotta get out of here!"* I exclaimed. Then

the cop did something outrageous. He reached over and felt my arm muscle and sneered, *"You got some pretty good guns there. I bet you can take care of yourself just fine."* If only it were true. I was terrified of the big city.

Just then I saw another bus that went to Long beach where my mom lived! So I sprinted to catch it lugging my purple doctors bag filled with props in one hand, a heavy disassembled table under my arm. In my other hand was an equipment case with my trusty anvil, sledgehammer and a bunch of other props. Under my arm was my purple suit jacket. No wonder my arm muscles were bulging. I was running at full gait to catch that bus. I was so flustered that I handed the bus driver my jaywalking ticket instead of my voucher. I dumped all my stuff in a vacant seat, found my voucher and proceeded to tell the driver

my whole pathetic story. *"I'm sorry,"* the driver said, *"But this bus won't get within five miles of where you want to go."* I felt like I was gonna puke at that moment, but what I said was, *"As close as you can, please."* As we drove on, I felt a very strange tingling sensation all over my body. I sat wondering, what had that guy slipped me?

"Here's your stop," the driver said. He exaggerated the actual distance. It was only about four miles, but it sure felt like a hundred. While I staggered along through the dark streets of Long Beach, not only was my body tingling with pain, but I was also carrying a bunch of cash that I'd been paid for my show. Luckily, my big purple hat probably scared off any would be muggers. Needless to say, I was quite fearful of being robbed. Yet somehow at a little after 3am, I knocked on my mother's door. When it opened, I

took two steps in and then — oblivion.

I awoke around 11:00am the next day. The first thing I noticed was that my entire body was still tingling. I also discovered I had three strange, large blisters on my arm. Over the next few days, I discovered what these were.

Remember that warm hill that I slept on? Well, it was been covered with poisonous plant life. From head to toe, I slept all over it. A magic plant that has the ability to transform the human body into a swollen mass of beet red tapioca.

If you haven't guessed, it was Poison Oak! After two months of scratching, when the last lesion was gone, I chirped a comedic line that I still use today, *"Back To Normal!"* Oh, how we suffer for our art! ♦

M I NEVER ISS

DAI VERNON

AS TOLD BY HOWARD HAMBURG

Larry Jennings, Mike Skinner, Max Maven, Ray Grismer and myself are all at The Magic Castle. The Professor, Dai Vernon is sitting at the corner stool at the main bar nearest the staircase all by himself. We are all around the bar just talking.

Out of nowhere, the Professor shouts, *"I Never Miss, I Never Miss."* Remember, he's all by himself with a deck of cards. So we really don't pay any attention to him. Once again he belts out, *"I never miss, I never miss."* So I said, *"Dai, what are you referring to?"* Dai replied, *"Howard, go ahead and select a card, select a card."* I did and showed everybody the Six of Hearts. Dai put it back into the deck. He continued, *"Give me a number between five and twenty."* I said, *"Eight."* He said, *"What, what,*

what?" Dai was looking at the cards trying to figure out how to get the Six of Hearts to the eighth position of the deck and stalling. He was holding the deck right up at eye level, so was not in any way trying to hide what he was doing. Remember, he's well into his eighties and still doing great magic. He began counting down to the number eight. One, two three, four, five, six, seven, eight. He asked, *"Howard, what was your card?"* I said, *"The Six of Hearts."* He turned it over and it was correct.

He repeated again, *"I never miss, I never miss."* I said, *"Professor, if you did miss, would you go out to dinner with Ray and I?"* We would like to have you join us. He replied, *"I never*

miss." I then said, *"Well, I'll make a bet with you. If you miss, will you go out to dinner with us?"* He said, *"Go ahead and select a card."* I selected

---

MAKE IT DIFFICULT FOR ME!

---

another card and showed everyone the Seven of Diamonds. It went back into the deck. Dai said, *"Make it difficult for me. Give me a number between five and twenty. Make it difficult, difficult, difficult."* I said, *"Okay, eleven."* He replied, *"What, what, what?"* Once again stalling and very out in the open. Then he began counting, *"One, two, three, four, five, six, seven, eight, nine, ten, eleven."* Without turning the card over to show me, he said, *"Howard, what was your card?"*

Since I wanted to go out to dinner with him, I said a completely different card to screw up the trick.

I answered, *"The King of Spades."* He turned the card over, and it was the damn King of Spades. What are the chances? He got it **wrong** and **right** all at the same time. A freak accident.

All of us were simply stunned at what just happened. We also didn't have the heart to tell him it really was wrong, so we let it be. Dai then got up off the stool, and began heading upstairs.

As he did, you heard his famous statement slowly fading into the background as he repeated over and over and over again, *"I told you, I never miss, I never miss."* ♦

Did You Know?

MAGIC IN THE AGES

When in the 4th century Christianity became the dominant religion of the Roman Empire, it turned against all magicians.

They were outlawed nearly everywhere. Later, in the Middle Ages, magicians were caught up in condemnations of witches, sorcerers, and devil worshipers.

They were often jailed and sometimes executed. Not until the Renaissance did it become possible for traveling entertainers, such as jugglers and other wonder workers, to perform before royalty, nobility, and even bishops if not always for the public.

By the 16th century there were professional magicians doing card tricks, reading minds, and making objects disappear.

HERE

I'M OVER

TONY SLYDINI

AS TOLD BY BILL WISCH

The famous Italian magician Tony Slydini did not have a driver's license and never drove when in the U.S. Living in Manhattan, it wasn't a huge problem. He would take trains or have friends and students take him around when he needed.

One evening, he had to go to Connecticut for a show. I was scheduled to pick him up outside of his apartment building on 45th street. I had done this dozens of times before. Tony usually waited for me in the *alcove-walkway* of his apartment building until he saw my beige Volkswagen pull up.

On this particular night, it was very cold and raining really hard. Tony was wearing a Fedora Hat and a long black trench coat to shield him from the inclement weather. His outfit made him look dangerous. Like a character out of a *Godfather* movie, you would hope to *never* meet in a dark alley.

> # LIKE SOME CHARACTER FROM THE GODFATHER MOVIE

On this night, I was nearing his apartment building, and I had to stop for a red light. But I was close enough to see him standing under the awning waiting for me. The rain was coming down viciously now, and without an umbrella you would be drenched in a few seconds. Coincidentally, there was **another** beige Volkswagen stopped directly in front of Tony at a red light.

He of course, thought **that** beige Volkswagen was mine and ran to it. He began pulling and pulling on the door handle, yelling, *"OPEN UP, OPEN UP!"* I was watching all this from just

OPEN UP!, OPEN UP!

a few feet away. I quickly got out of my car and shouted, *"Tony, Tony, I'm over here. Over here!"*

But the thundering sound of rain drowned out my words. He was so caught up in the moment, he didn't hear me. He continued shouting and yanking at the door handle, getting more agitated by the second. The car door would not open. The people in that car had no idea what the hell was going on?

They probably thought, *"This Italian guy is trying to carjack us!"* I watched the horror these people experienced. It was like watching a scary movie, except I was the director, or at least the

accidental initiator of it. Because of city lighting, I could easily see everyone's shadow through their back window. They were horrified. All tightly pressed up against the driver's side with their arms up in total fear.

Here's this guy, yelling at the top of his lungs, *"OPEN UP, OPEN UP, LET ME IN!"* and trying desperately to get into their car. Finally, the light changed and I was able to pull up in front of Tony. When he saw my car, he looked really confused. Two beige Volkswagens?

Then a light bulb went off in his head, and he realized what just happened. He had made a big mistake. He quickly got

into my car and calmly asked me how I was. I was laughing so hard, I couldn't answer him.

He smiled at me and said, *"I thoughta you wasa crazy notta to letta me ina."* We laughed about it all the way to Connecticut.

Though the entire scene only lasted about thirty seconds, I'm sure it was an eternity for the occupants of that car.

Today, I still laugh when I think what must have been going through those poor folk's minds on that dark, rainy wet night in New York City when they were attacked by a little Italian man. ♦

A BIG SURPRISE

HARRY & GAY BLACKSTONE

AS TOLD BY GAY BLACKSTONE

My husband, Harry Blackstone Jr. and I were performing in Chicago, IL. It was December of 1992, and needless to say, it was very cold outside. We were at the Chicago Auditorium Theater which is a very famous venue and seats 5000 people.

Our show was going great and our next illusion involved an elephant. The elephant was escorted out by his trainer and arrived center stage. Harry was positioned in front of it, I was at stage left, and our eight dancers were at stage right. We began raising walls all around the elephant. One from behind it and two from the sides.

The front panel was also raised, but this panel has a screen on it, therefore, you could see the elephant inside at all times. Once the last panel was raised,

> # THE ELEPHANT IS GONE! WELL, SORT OF...

Harry told the audience not to blink. He then clapped his hands and said, *"GO!"*

All the panels that surrounded the elephant dropped, and the elephant was completely GONE! Or was it? Because of the cold weather, the elephant could not eat its regular diet. After all, we were in the city and feed stores were scarce. We substituted the elephant's normal diet of grain with another we found locally. Well, this new feed really upset its stomach. When Harry clapped his hands and said, *"GO,"* the trainer also shouted loudly, *"OH, NO!!!"*

Yes, the elephant vanished, but not completely yet. You see, in its place it left a huge, I mean HUGE, pile of (*how can I say*) POOP! Uncomfortable silence overwhelmed the theater. We all just stared at it for a moment and thought, *"Now what?"* Being the consummate professional, Harry in his best speaking voice, immediately broke the silence and announced, *"Well, if there was any doubt that it was not a **REAL** elephant, well here's your proof!"* Everyone on-stage lost it, and everyone in the audience lost it. I think everyone laughed what seemed to be minutes straight.

A few moments later one of the dancers came out from backstage with a BIG Golden Shovel and began cleaning up the mess, in front of the entire audience.

Once again even more laughter. I do not think anyone in that audience will ever forget that night. I know I never will. ♦

Did You Know?

MAGIC BOOKS

The first magic book in English came out in 1612.

Reginald Scot issued the book, *The Discovery of Witchcraft* to expose the sleight-of-hand artists of his time.

The original book is still in existence and is owned by a private collector.

The trick went tragically *wrong* when Chung was performing in the Wood Green Empire, London, on March 23, 1918.

— READY, AIM FIRE *page 233*

Better Safe Than SORRY

BILLY McCOMB

AS TOLD BY IVAN AMODEI

Billy McComb is considered a legend in magic, and so is the story surrounding one of the effects he performed. It was also one of Billy's favourite stories to tell.

The effect is called the SANDS OF THE DESERT. To accomplish this effect, each performance of it utilizes multiple condoms. Yes, condoms.

Billy was booked for a six week run in a small theatre in England. He had to do eight shows a week and each show used up three condoms.

He figured for the length of the run at the theatre he was going to need 144 condoms or a GROSS. He arrived in the town on a Friday afternoon, he thought he would spend his weekend preparing all his props (*condoms*) for the entire length of his run at the theatre.

He headed to the local pharmacy of this quaint village to buy the condoms. He walked in and casually asked the young pimpled-faced clerk, *"Hello, I need a GROSS of condoms. Do you have them in stock?"* The clerk looked inquisitively at the older, gray-haired, gentlemen before him, paused, as he evaluated the situation, his face reflected a look of wonder.

He then muttered, *"Right. Yes, ummm, we do have, ummm, a gross, yes, right,"* and handed him the case of condoms. Billy eagerly headed back to his hotel room and spent the remainder of the weekend preparing the condoms for the shows. When he got to the last inside box, he realized that he was two

YES, CONDOMS

condoms short. On Monday morning, Billy stormed back into the pharmacy. He was by now extremely aggravated by this inconvenience.

Unable to hide his irritation, he barked at the lanky, adolescent clerk, *"Hey, remember me, I came here Friday and bought 144 condoms from you. Well, there were only 142!"*

The clerk brushed his red curly hair back, while he scratched his head, looking intently at the old man before him, who had instantly become his idol and said, *"Well, I hope it didn't ruin your weekend."* ♦

About the Author

What just happened? That is the question you will ask yourself during and after you see Ivan Amodei perform. He is like a prize fighter — light on his feet with a punch that you'll never see coming. He will fool you. Badly. And he'll do it with a smile. And, the crazy thing is, you'll be smiling too. It's as if you were in the rink with Mohammed Ali. He enters the stage hitting hard and entertaining you all along the way.

At first, you think that's just his hook — his smile. But once you get to know Ivan, you'll realize that he is never without it. It's infectious. It spreads to everyone. I know this because I see it in every member of his audience. And, I see it in myself. I don't believe I've been in his presence without a smile of my own. As an audience member, you can't help but be mesmerized by him. There are very few magicians that can keep a performance fresh, seemingly spontaneous, and energized, over and over again, while entertaining the pants off you too. Ivan is one of these few. I think his secret is his true love for this art, and more importantly for life.

He is undeniably one of the best in this field. He is also undeniably a happy soul. That joy filters into all that he does (*including this book*), and you'll see it, in full glory, when he's on stage. But as you peel away the onion, you'll begin to see the layers that make up this man.

He has many talents. Yes, he's an expert magician/entertainer, but he's also a skilled graphic designer (*just look inside*), a loving, happy husband, and a great father. Now add ***Author*** to that list too.

Which brings me to this book. It's one of the most unique pieces on magic and magicians that has ever been achieved.

All his experience, talents and knowledge on *"how to present"* magic and/or a story has been funneled into the creation of this book. And no one could be more qualified to create it than Ivan. It's not only visually appealing, but contains tons of content too. There's never a boring second. And extreme attention to *every* detail. Exactly what you would expect of a single performance from him. It's fantastic.

Lastly and most importantly, I'm thrilled I'm able to call Ivan my friend.

Jonathan Levit
Magician / Actor / Host
www.jonathanlevit.com

CREDITS & ACKNOWLEDGEMENTS

CREDITS & ACKNOWLEDGEMENTS

CREDITS & ACKNOWLEDGEMENTS

CREDITS & ACKNOWLEDGEMENTS

CREDITS & ACKNOWLEDGEMENTS